Cook IT

version 1.0

OTHER LOTUS TITLES

Street Foods of India
The Landour Cookbook
Nutritive Cooking for Children
Moti Mahal's Tandoori Trail
Continental Cuisine for the Indian Palate
The Indian Vegetarian Cookbook

CHEFS' SPECIAL SERIES

Awadhi Kitchen
Bengali Kitchen
Chinese Kitchen
Chicken Delight
Curries and Rice
Delhi Kitchen
Dum Cuisine
Favourite Indian Desserts
Goan Kitchen
Gujarati Kitchen
Iyer Kitchen
Kerala Kitchen
Kashmiri Kitchen
Low Calorie Desserts
Marwari Kitchen
Nepalese Kitchen
Punjabi Kitchen
Parsi Kitchen
Rajasthani Kitchen
Seafood Platter
Snacks and Desserts
South Indian Kitchen
Thai Kitchen
Tikkas and Kebabs
Vegetarian Fiesta

Cook IT
version 1.0

Kiran Rao

LOTUS COLLECTION
ROLI BOOKS

For an interactive experience visit www.cook-it.co.in. You will find discussion forums, photographs and new recipes updated weekly.

Lotus Collection 2010

First published in 2010
An imprint of Roli Books Pvt. Ltd.
M-75, G.K. II Market, New Delhi 110 048
Phones: ++91 (011) 2921 2271, 40682000. Fax: ++91 (011) 2921 7185
E-mail: info@rolibooks.com; Website: rolibooks.com
Also at Bangalore, Chennai, Jaipur, Kolkata & Mumbai

Design: Supriya Saran

ISBN: 978-81-7436-712-9

Typeset in Myriad Pro by Roli Books Pvt. Ltd.
and printed at Anubha Printers, Noida

I wish to thank my wife, Vimmi,
for patiently eating everything I cook,
without complaining, and for being supportive
of my efforts to innovate in the kitchen

Cooking is a great way to test your project management skills as it requires you to conceive solutions, estimate resources accurately, organize tasks, execute well, test results and deliver an optimized product to demanding stakeholders. You also are challenged to improve the process every time you repeat it and exercise innovation to keep your stakeholders happy.

The total direct employment in the Indian IT-ITES sector is estimated to have grown by approximately a million, from 1,29,3000 in FY 2006 to a 2,236,614 in FY 2009.* This book is targeted at these millions of Information Technology workers who toil everyday to keep the Indian software juggernaut plowing on and on into global stardom. Many of these millions are far away from home, from their mothers and the kitchens of their homes where hot delicious meals are churned out on pre-determined schedules or, as IBM would call it, On-Demand. For many who find themselves alone for the first time, it's always a challenge setting up a kitchen and beginning to do something realistic and reasonable in it. Some of the language and terms used in this book are borrowed from the IT industry, which gives the reader a familiar terrain to tread on by reason of association. Concepts from the SDLC (Software Development Life Cycle) and Project Management are used to explain the processes involved in preparing a meal.

* NASSCOM, 2008-2009

Contents

- INTRODUCTION TO DDLC 9
  - DDLC Stages
  - Dish Architecture
- STARTING A KITCHEN 15
  - Organizational Process Assets
- MAIN COURSE
  - **Curry Dishes**
    - Sada Dal 22
    - Tadka Dal 23
    - Sambar 25
    - Rasam 27
    - Chana Dal 29
    - Dal Makhni 31
    - Chana Masala 34
    - Rajma Masala 37
    - Lobiya Masala 40
    - Vegetable Kofta 43
    - Palak Paneer 46
    - Bhein aur Aloo Masala 48
    - Anda Masala 50
    - Gucchi Matar ki Subzi 52
    - Arvi Tamatar Masala 54
    - Paneer Butter Masala 57
    - Vadia aur Aloo Rasedaar 59
    - Matar Paneer 61
    - Aloo Matar Rasedaar 63
    - Bhindi Kadhi 65
- **Dry Dishes**
  - Bhindi Fry 68
  - Baingan Aloo 70
  - Bharwan Karela 72
  - Jhatpat Paneer 74
  - Kurkuri Arvi 76
  - Bandh Gobi ki Subzi 78
  - Aloo Gobi 80
  - Bharwan Bhindi 82
  - Masaledaar Kaccha Kela 84
  - Bhein Mazedaar 86
  - Aloo Beans 88
  - Tindora Fry 90
  - Besani Hara Pyaz 92
  - Anda Bhurji 94
  - Turai ki Subzi 96
  - Bharwan Baingan 98
  - Bhuni Borboti 100
  - Pyaz Patti 102
  - Milijuli Subzi 104
  - Dahi Bhindi 106
  - Dum Aloo 108
  - Bharwan Mirchi 111
  - Bharwan Baingan Kishti 113
  - Kele ke Phool ki Subzi 115
  - Karela Fry 117
  - Bharwan Shimla Mirch 119
  - Dahi Lauki 121
  - Bhuna Gajar 123
  - Baingan Bharta 124
  - Kele ka Tana 126
  - Punjabi Tinda 128

→ RICE

Sada Chawal	132
Nimbu ka Pulihora	134
Tamatar ka Pulao	136
Imli ka Pulihora	138
Matar Pulao	140
Vangi Baht	142
Thayir Sadam	144

→ BREADS

Sada Roti	148
Sada Paratha	150
Aloo Paratha	152
Mooli Paratha	154
Puri	156
Missi Roti	158

→ RAITAS

Khira Gajar Raita	162
Aloo Pyaz Raita	164
Shimla Mirch Raita	166

→ CHUTNEYS

Pyaz ki Chutney	168
Nariyal ki Chutney	170
Nimbu ki Chutney	172
Dhaniya Pudine ki Chutney	174

Introduction to DDLC

This book is outlined into chapters that walk the reader through the process of setting up a basic kitchen, gathering essential ingredients and finally, getting started with the cooking. The general approach to cooking a dish is similar to a combination of Software Development Life Cycle (SDLC) used to develop software products and Project Management as advocated by PMI (Project Management Institute). For the rest of this book, we will consider cooking a dish as a project.

The SDLC methodology follows defined stages of:

Feasibility Study	Can we do this project?
Requirements Analysis	What does the customer want from this project?
Design	Conceptual solution to meet customer's requirement
Development	Build the solution
Testing	Test the solution to verify it meets customer's requirement
Implementation	Move solution into production
Maintenance	Maintain solution to continue meeting customer's expectations

The PMI advocated Project Management methodology follows the defined five process groups:

Initiating Process Group	Formal authorization to start a project
Planning Process Group	Plan and manage the project for successful completion
Executing Process Group	Complete the defined work
Monitoring & Control Process Group	Monitor to identify problems early and take corrective action

Closing Process Group	Hand-off completed project or terminate cancelled project

A combination of these two globally recognized methodologies in the kitchen will yield what I call the Dish Development Life Cycle (DDLC). DDLC stages include:

INITIATION STAGE

Meal Analysis	Stakeholder review of dishes to prepare
Feasibility Study	Review of skills and ingredients required to prepare dishes
High-Level Project Overview	Summary of dishes at 40,000 feet view

PLANNING STAGE

Project Schedule	Estimation of time to cook dishes
Inventory and Procurement	Capacity planning and procurement of ingredients
Quality Assurance	Implementation of planned quality measures

EXECUTION STAGE

Execution	Chopping, slicing, dicing, frying, boiling and mixing
Testing and Optimization	Variations of core ingredients and spices

TESTING AND DEPLOYMENT STAGE

Quality Testing	Taste the dishes to verify quality standards are met
Suggested Deployment	What to serve the dish with

CLOSING STAGE

Maintenance	Store leftovers
Closure	Wash and put away empty vessels and utensils

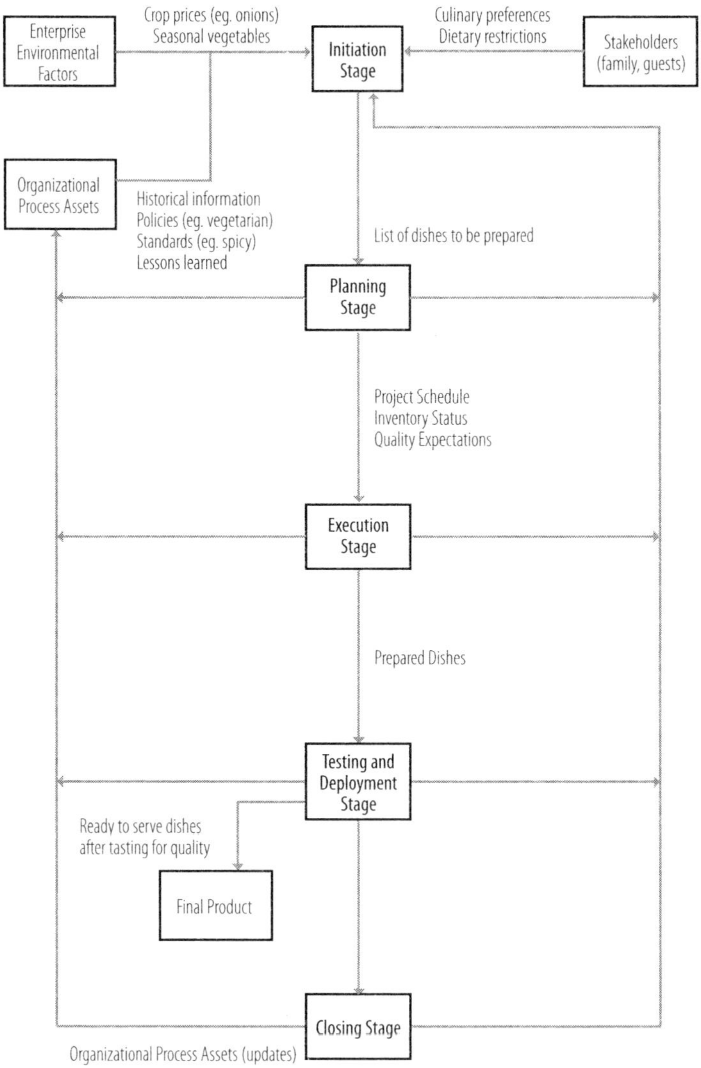
Enterprise Environmental Factors
Crop prices (eg. onions)
Seasonal vegetables
Initiation Stage
Culinary preferences
Dietary restrictions
Stakeholders (family, guests)
Organizational Process Assets
Historical information
Policies (eg. vegetarian)
Standards (eg. spicy)
Lessons learned
List of dishes to be prepared
Planning Stage
Project Schedule
Inventory Status
Quality Expectations
Execution Stage
Prepared Dishes
Testing and Deployment Stage
Ready to serve dishes after tasting for quality
Final Product
Closing Stage
Organizational Process Assets (updates)

▸▸ DDLC STAGES

High-Level Project Overview

At this stage you will perform your due diligence on the dish and its key ingredients. You will learn a little about their origin, history, nutrition value, etc. These pieces of knowledge should quickly help you decide if this is the project you want to take up.

Project Schedule

The approx.imate time required to complete the project is stated in this stage. You will also learn if you can complete the task in a linear mode (start the next task after completing the earlier task) or in parallel mode (start the next task before completing the first task).

Inventory & Procurement

In cooking, project selection is often driven by what raw material is found in the refrigerator, as versus what the palate desires. Unless you are the kind who goes shopping for the exact vegetable you want to see in your curry, even if there is another vegetable sitting in your fridge shelf for a week (perhaps, changing a little colour too). The curry at your dining table is often dictated by what you already shopped for. At this stage of meal preparation, you take stock of what resources you have at your disposal to execute the meal project in a manner satisfactory to its key stakeholders (your tongue and stomach).

Quality Control

In this stage you perform the mandatory pre-requisites with the procured inventory to meet the expected quality standard of the dish. Quality control examples include:

- Washing rice, lentils, pulses, and vegetables
- How to store certain chopped vegetables to prevent oxidation
- How to correctly soak lentils and pulses
- Guidance in using certain kitchen instruments like pressure cooker

Execution

This is the sweat stage of the meal preparation process, where your clothes get stained, hands get greasy and your skin smells of *masala*. It's important to perform a

WBS (Work Breakdown Structure) at this stage to help you better organize work packages you will be required to perform in parallel. Major routines include:

- Chopping of vegetables
- Cooking
- Preparing seasoning which includes scraping ginger, peeling garlic cloves, slitting green chillies, de-stalking curry leaves, etc
- Soaking and extracting juice from wet spices like tamarind or lemons
- Integration – bringing it all together

Testing and Optimization

At this stage you will taste (test) the prepared dish for consistency, desired taste, desired look (even if you are not entertaining guests you should be bothered with the look of the dish, remember when your mother said, 'a feast for the eyes is a feast for the stomach') and perform any adjustments required. Most frequent failures occur in salt and spice levels or degree of wetness/dryness desired. I have also dug into my database of R&D results and made some suggested variations like replacing certain ingredients with others; this is where ones' imagination comes in handy.

Suggested Deployment

In this last stage of a DDLC, you will determine how the dish is served. I have made a few suggestions, but in reality you may have an infinite array of combinations to try and your liking could very well differ from mine.

▸▸ DISH ARCHITECTURE

Unlike western cuisine where there is ample chance that a single dish may not take centerstage, in Indian cuisine you will find various categories of dishes with different architectures surrounding one or two central dishes, I call these central dishes as Foundation Dishes. A good meal will consist of a large foundation dish (like rice or *roti*), some dry vegetables (*bhindi* fry, *bharwan baingan*) and at least one curry dish (like *sambar*, *kadhi*). Common architecture types include:

Dry fry: In this method of preparation, you fry the ingredients with oil in an open pan so any moisture inside the vegetable evaporates and does not permeate back into the dish. The key point to note is absolutely no water, not even the natural water content from inside the ingredients.

Semi-wet: In this method of preparation, you fry the ingredients in oil but allow for moisture inclusion, either by adding water or retaining the vegetable's natural water content in the dish by covering the pan with a lid.

Wet: In this type of preparation, you add copious quantities of water which is retained in the dish making it gravy. Typically approximately 50 per cent of this dish is water.

▸▸ GOLDEN COOKING RULES (to swear by)

Cooking is not a born skill, some people are not 'just better at it' than others. Just like Java or Oracle, you have to learn and use it frequently enough to become fluent at it.

Most don't get it right the first time. However, unlike office work cooking allows more freedom to make mistakes and there is no penalty for getting it wrong.

There is no fixed recipe for most dishes. Use experience first and then let imagination take over.

For experienced cooks, the eye is the measure and not the spoon. Use the ingredients quantities provided in this book as guidance. Exact quantities will ultimately be based on your preference.

Starting a Kitchen

A good well-stocked kitchen is the starting point for great culinary experiences. Essential crockery and equipment you will need to start a kitchen include:

Measuring jug
Tablespoons
Teaspoons
Peeler
Masher
Mortar and pestle
Rolling pin
Scissors

Lemon squeezer
Cooking gas and stove
Large non-stick frying pan with lid
Large non-stick casserole pot with lid
Non-stick flat pan (Omni *tawa*)
Medium non-stick saucepan with lid
10" thermoware container
Grinder / Blender

Measuring spoons

5-litre pressure cooker

Casserole pots and saucepans with lids

Colander

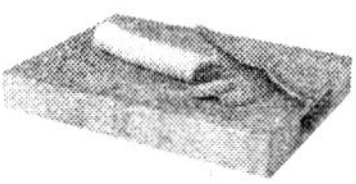

Chopping board

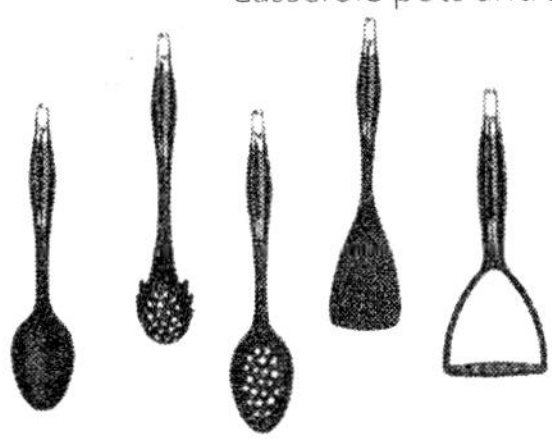

Ladle spoon set

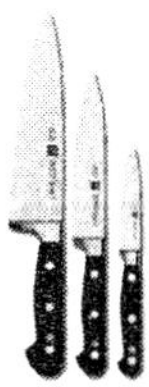

Knife set

▸▸ ORGANIZATIONAL PROCESS ASSETS

Organization process assets are lessons learnt from previous experience stored in well documented, classified and categorized manner using an MIS system such as Microsoft Office. The most valuable, reproducible, repeatable processes and lessons become organizational best practices shared among departments for the benefit of greater success in on-time on-budget project delivery. Here I am granting you access to my repository of best practices which I store and update using Microsoft Word and Excel.

Best Practices – Inventory Management

The common cooking ingredients that I have used in this book are listed below. There are many more spices available for use in traditional Indian cuisine, like cloves, basil, fenugreek, fennel, bay leaf, star anise, and cardamom, but I have used these spices sparingly and hence they are not listed as essential. As your expertise in cooking builds, you may feel free to start experimenting with them.

Grains, Flours and Cooking Oils

Basmati rice
Wholewheat flour
Gram flour (*besan* or chickpea flour)
Cooking oil (sunflower or peanut)
Mustard oil

Lentils, Nuts and Pulses

Yellow lentils (*tur, toor* or *tuvar dal*)
Black gram (*urad dal*)
Chickpeas (*kabuli chana*)
Bengal Gram (*chana dal*)
Split green gram (*moong dal*)
Red kidney beans (*rajma*)
Black-eyed beans (*lobiya*)
Peanuts (*moongphalli*)
Cashew nuts (*kaju*)

Dry spices

Garam masala powder
Red chilli powder (*lal mirch*)
Red chillies
Turmeric powder (*haldi*)
Coriander powder (*dhaniya*)
Cumin powder (*jeera*)
Dry mango powder (*amchur*)
Tandoori *masala* powder
Andhra peanut powder
Sambar powder
Rasam powder
Vangi baht powder
Dry fenugreek leaf powder (*kasoori methi*)
Asafoetida powder (*hing*)
Mustard seeds (*rai*)
Carom (*ajwain seeds*)
Common salt

Black pepper (*kali mirch*)
Sun-dried dumplings (*vadia*)

Vegetables

Okra (*bhindi*)
Eggplant (*baingan*)
Cabbage (*band gobi*)
Cauliflower (*phool gobi*)
Potato (*aloo*)
Bitter gourd (*karela*)
Ridge gourd (*turai*)
Snake gourd (*lauki*)
Mushroom (*khumb*)
Colocasia (*arvi*)
Peas (*matar*)
Green banana (*hara kela*)
Banana stem
Banana flower
Spring onion (*hara pyaz*)
Onion stalk
Flat bean (*velore*)
String bean
Ivy gourd (*tindora*)
Carrots (*gajar*)
Tomato (*tamatar*)
Onion (*pyaz*)
Lotus stem (*bhein*)
Apple gourd (*tinda*)
Cucumber (*khira*)
White radish (*mooli*)
Spinach (*palak*)
Capsicum (*Shimla mirch*)
Anaheim peppers
Cayenne peppers

Wet Spices & Herbs

Ginger (*adrak*)
Garlic (*lasan*)
Coriander leaves (*dhaniya*)
Mint leaves (*pudina*)
Fenugreek leaves (*methi*)
Curry leaves (*kadhi patta*)
Green chillies (*hara mirch*)
Lemon juice (*nimbu*)
Tamarind paste (*imli*)

Dairy & Farm Products

Yoghurt (*dahi*)
Milk
Cream
Butter
Clarified butter (*ghee*)
Cottage Cheese (*paneer*)
Eggs

Ingredient Storage Practices

- Store spices, lentils and grains in clean transparent plastic or glass bottles in an easily accessible area in the kitchen. Don't penny-pinch on buying a few jars for storing these ingredients, you will be surprised to know ants and weevils eat pretty much anything we eat. Label them, the effort is worth it (you could type up an excel sheet of inventory but accessing it in the kitchen will be an issue). Lesser the time spent searching for ingredients, better the chance of making a tasty dish.

- Try shopping every weekend for supplies, not once a month or Just-In-Time. Analyze your habits and decide how many days you eat at home. Buy enough vegetables and wet spices to cover these days. Grains, lentils and dry spices can be stocked in larger quantities and hence do not require frequent shopping for.
- When refrigerating vegetables, wash and snip off their appendages before placing in the fridge. This action will lend longer storage life to the vegetables as the appendages start to rot first, triggering off the rotting process of the vegetable itself and surrounding vegetables too.

Best Practices – Execution

- Always chop or peel all vegetables before starting to cook. One of the easiest ways of ruining a dish is by getting busy chopping vegetables while a dish is already cooking on the flame.
- Ensure all the ingredients for every dish are readily available before starting to cook; one more reason why dishes get ruined is because they are left cooking while the cook goes to shop for the missing ingredient from a nearby store. Yes, everyone thinks they can come back in two minutes.
- If you find yourself with a few minutes of free time, use it to wash any dirty pans/utensils (however, don't get carried away and start a cleaning frenzy!). You will avoid having a stockpile to wash at the end of the meal preparation when you are most tired. This also ensures you have the utensils readily available in case you need to use them repeatedly at different stages of the meal preparation process.
- Keep a small dish on the stove counter to place the stirring spoons. You will avoid getting turmeric-laden oil stains on the stove that will prove a pain to clean later.
- Keep the kitchen well ventilated. When you perform a seasoning (*tadka* or *thalimpu*), the smoke and fumes will inevitably choke you and you will sprint for fresh air. This will result in the seasoning getting burnt.
- When using pressure cooker, always ensure that you do not let it stay on heat for so long that it runs out of water inside. If this happen, the safety valve will blow and could seriously hurt you and the surroundings by spraying ultra-hot contents through the safety valve hole. Strictly follow the guidelines in the recipes.

When you switch off the flame under a pressure cooker, do not remove the valve immediately. Wait for the steam to condense before removing the valve; this usually takes about 15 minutes.

- Do not add wet chopped vegetables directly to hot oil; the oil will splatter on hands and body causing severe burns. Result? Burnt vegetables and blistered skin. Ensure to shake water off washed vegetables and wipe them with a clean towel.
- Beware when mixing vegetables in cooking, not all vegetables cook at the same rate. Example, spinach and potato (spinach cooks in a few minutes, potatoes take much longer). Vegetables must be added into the cooking pan in a staggered manner so that at all vegetables are equally cooked.
- Wash your hands frequently with a liquid soap when cooking, you never know when you will unconsciously scratch your nose or rub your eyes after chopping a caustic vegetable like green chilli. Why liquid soap? If you use a solid soap bar, the harsh elements tends to stick to the bar and burn you when you wash next time.
- When you decide to cook, don't take a shower and start. Indian cuisine often leaves an olfaction clinging to the body. Finish cooking, and then go take a shower, especially if you have a date coming for dinner!

Best Practices – Preparing Seasoning

- Indian seasoning generally uses the following ingredients: oil, mustard seeds, cumin seeds, Bengal gram, peanuts, green chillies, ginger/garlic, curry leaves, asafoetida, turmeric powder, and other dry spices. Not all ingredients are required in every seasoning, but the order prevails.
- Always chop and keep aside any of the required ingredients for seasoning.
- Not everyone loves chewing ginger but they can appreciate the ginger flavour. When chopping it you can keep the size of the pieces relatively large so that people who don't like chewing it can remove it from their servings.
- When heating oil, do not heat to an extent that the oil begins to fume. If the oil fumes it will burn any ingredient you add in, thus destroying the delicate flavours.
- When you add mustard seeds to hot oil, the mustard must splutter instantaneously. If it doesn't, then the oil is not hot enough to start the addition of ingredients for an effective seasoning. If mustard is not allowed to splutter, it will not release its flavour into the oil and thus its addition becomes futile.

- Always add asafoetida at the last few seconds of keeping the flame alive, it has a very delicate flavour and prolonged exposure to hot oil will kill its essence.
- Also add curry leaves about a minute before shutting off the flame. They cook quickly and I don't like crisp fried curry leaves in my seasoning.
- Do not add ginger-garlic paste to hot oil, it's a wet spice and will cause splattering which could be injurious to you. Add at least one major vegetable, usually onions, before adding the ginger-garlic paste.

Best Practices – Measurements & Capacity Planning

Most cookbooks require you to measure solids and liquids by grams and litres. Now it's unlikely that measuring devices for this purpose are found in a rookie techie's kitchen (heck, even I didn't have one till much later). So keeping this in mind I have made it easy for you by using a standard cup and a set of plastic spoons you will find in any decent supermarket.

For Rice and Dals

- Buy a small cup (200 gm) of Nestle or Amul yoghurt from your local store or supermarket. Eat the yoghurt and wash the cup.
- One cup of raw white rice measured using this cup, when cooked, will feed one person.
- One cup of raw yellow lentil measured using this cup, when cooked, will make enough *dal* for two people.
- 200 gm measure using yoghurt cup

For Spices and Oils

You can buy this set of four spoons in a supermarket, in the kitchen section. I suggest you get one from a reputed manufacturer so it's accurate and lasts a long time in your possession. As you become more experienced in cooking, you will find yourself using your hands more and these spoons less. However, when you eventually venture into something new like Chinese cuisine, you will need them again.

When using these spoons to measure spice or oil, always use level spoonfuls. Do not get excited and add heaped spoonfuls as this could destroy the taste of the dish.

All the recipes in this book are prepared for either 2 or 4 persons. I am guessing you will not like the idea of cooking everyday (to begin with), so I planned the quantities so that the dishes will last you for more than one meal.

Curry Dishes

SADA DAL

Basic Red Gram Lentil

Serves 2

High-Level Project Overview

This protein powerhouse is a great foundation dish for Indian IT engineers. Like plain rice is a chassis for all flavoured rice dishes, plain *dal* forms the chassis for various flavoured *dal* ones. It is also the base of some more complex gravy dishes (eg. *sambar*).

▸▸ Project Schedule

10 minutes in linear execution mode

▸▸ Inventory & Procurement

1 cup / 200 gm Split red gram (*tur dal*)

1 tbsp / 15 gm Ghee

1 tsp / 5 gm Turmeric (*haldi*) powder

1 tsp / 5 gm Salt

▸▸ Quality Assurance

- Wash *dal* in running water twice and drain before cooking.
- Wait for cooker to depressurize before opening.

▸▸ Execution

- Place *dal* in pressure cooker and add water 1:2 ratio.
- Add ghee, turmeric powder, and salt. Pressure cook till eight whistles.

▸▸ Testing & Optimization

- Split red gram can be replaced with split green gram.

▸▸ Suggested Deployment

This dish can be eaten with *roti* and vegetables like *bharwan bhindi* (see p. 82), or *bharwan karela* (see p. 72). In South Indian states like Andhra Pradesh plain thick *dal* is often eaten with hot rice and homemade butter (from churned yoghurt).

TADKA DAL

Tempered Red Gram Lentil — Serves 2

> **High-Level Project Overview**
>
> Since plain *dal* can become boring unless mixed with a copious amounts of ghee (unhealthy stuff for IT folks who get little or no exercise), it's often mixed with a vegetable to spike up the taste. Flavoured *dals* bridge the gap between plain *dal* and complex gravy dishes like *kadhi* and *sambar*. We will prepare this dish with tomatoes and split red gram, but remember this dish can be any lentil flavoured with almost any vegetable.

Project Schedule

20 minutes in parallel execution modes

Inventory & Procurement

1 cup / 200 gm Split red gram (*tur dal*)
4 Tomatoes, medium-sized
1 tsp / 5 gm Turmeric (*haldi*) powder
1 tsp / 5 gm Salt
3 tbsp / 45 ml Vegetable oil
1 tsp / 3 gm Mustard seeds (*rai*)
5 Garlic (*lasan*) cloves
2 Green chillies
¼ tsp Asafoetida (*hing*) powder
2 stalks Curry leaves (*kadhi patta*)
¼ cup / 15 gm Green coriander (*hara dhaniya*) leaves

Quality Assurance

- Wash *dal*, tomatoes, green chillies, green coriander, and curry leaves in running water.
- Curry leaves must look fresh and green. Old curry leaves will be dry and stiff, avoid these.
- Wait for cooker to depressurize before opening.

Execution

Subroutine 1 – Preparing dal (15 minutes)

- Chop tomatoes into quarters.

- Place *dal* and tomato in pressure cooker and add water 1:2 ratio.
- Add turmeric powder and salt.
- Pressure cook till eight whistles on high flame. Set aside.

Subroutine 2 – Preparing seasoning (4 minutes)

- Slightly mash garlic by hitting them once with a flat utensil; slit green chillies lengthwise. Set aside.
- Heat the oil in a casserole pot on high flame for 1 minute.
- Add mustard seeds and allow them to splutter.
- Add garlic and green chillies; fry for 1 minute stirring frequently.
- Add asafoetida and curry leaves. Stir well for 30 seconds.

Subroutine 3 – Integration (1 minute)

- To the cooked *dal*, add the seasoning and mix well.
- Garnish with chopped green coriander leaves.

▸▸ Testing & Optimization

- Replace the tomatoes with any vegetable as desired such as spinach, gongura, yellow cucumber, green mango, etc.
- To get a tangy taste, add juice of half a lemon.
- You can replace oil with ghee.

▸▸ Suggested Deployment

Tadka dal can be eaten with rice, *roti* and dry fried vegetables like *kurkuri arvi* (see p. 76) or *aloo gobi* (see p. 80)

SAMBAR

Vegetables in Tempered Red Gram — Serves 2

High-Level Project Overview

For me, this dish is the nectar of South India. The copious quantities of tamarind used in *sambar* makes it a very heart-healthy dish as tartaric acid (main ingredient in tamarind) is known to clean out the fatty gunk that accumulates in our arteries.

▸▸ Project Schedule

42 minutes in parallel execution mode

▸▸ Inventory & Procurement

1 cup / 200 gm Split red gram (*tur dal*)
2 Onions, large
250 gm Okra (*bhindi*)
8 Garlic (*lasan*) cloves
3 tbsp / 45 ml Vegetable oil
1 tsp / 3 gm Mustard seeds (*rai*)
1 tsp / 3 gm Cumin (*jeera*) seeds
2 stalks Curry leaves (*kadhi patta*)
½ tsp / 2½ gm Asafoetida (*hing*) powder
1 tsp / 5 gm Turmeric (*haldi*) powder
1 tbsp / 15 gm Tamarind (*imli*) paste
2 tbsp / 15 gm *Sambar* powder
2 tsp / 10 gm Salt
¼ cup / 15 gm Green coriander (*hara dhaniya*) leaves

▸▸ Quality Assurance

- If buying the unpackaged okra, bend the ends to test for tenderness. The end should snap when bent. If it bends all the way, the okra has become soft with age.
- Curry leaves must look fresh and green. Avoid old curry leaves that are dry and stiff.
- Wash *dal*, onions, okra, curry leaves, and coriander leaves in running water

▸▸ Execution

Subroutine 1 – Preparing dal (10 minutes)

- Prepare the *dal* as described on page 22, without the turmeric powder and salt.
- Mash into soft paste and set aside.

Subroutine 2 – Preparing tamarind gravy (35 minutes)

- Cut onions into quarters, chop okra into 2" pieces, and mash garlic by hitting them once with a flat utensil. Set aside.
- Heat the oil in a casserole pot on high flame for 1 minute.
- Add mustard seeds and allow them to splutter.
- Add cumin seeds and fry for 20-25 seconds.
- Add garlic, curry leaves, and asafoetida. Fry for 15 seconds.
- Add onions, okra, and turmeric powder. Fry for 10 minutes stirring constantly.
- Add 6 cups water, tamarind paste, *sambar* powder, and salt. Lid the pot and boil for 20 minutes over medium flame.

Subroutine 3 – Integration (5 minutes)

- Add the *dal* to the tamarind gravy and cook for further 5 minutes.
- Garnish with chopped green coriander leaves.

▸▸ Testing & Optimization

- A variety of vegetables can be added to the *sambar*. I have often replaced okra with any one of the following: carrots, radish, potato, eggplant, etc.

▸▸ Suggested Deployment

Sambar is eaten with rice or *idlis* in South Indian states like Andhra Pradesh and Tamil Nadu. Since it has a strong flavour it's best eaten with rice and mild vegetables like *bhuna gajar* (see p.123) or *bandh gobi ki subzi* (see p. 78).

RASAM

Hot Spicy South Indian Tomato Soup Serves 2

High-Level Project Overview

Rasam is uttered in a venerable tone in South Indian states; it's drunk as an appetizer, as a medicine and as part of a meal. Different states of India have different variations, some add grated coconut powder and some add jaggery. I love the good old plain *rasam* with fried garlic!

▶▶ Project Schedule

15 minutes in linear execution mode

▶▶ Inventory & Procurement

2 Tomatoes
2 tsp / 10 gm Tamarind (*imli*) paste
2 tbsp / 30 ml Vegetable oil
1 tsp / 3 gm Mustard seeds (*rai*)
1 tsp / 3 gm Cumin (*jeera*) seeds
1 stalk Curry leaves (*kadhi patta*)
8 Garlic (*lasan*) cloves
¼ tsp Asafoetida (*hing*) powder
2 tsp / 10 gm Salt
1 tbsp / 7½ gm *Rasam* powder

▶▶ Quality Assurance

- Wash the tomatoes and curry leaves in running water.
- Curry leaves must look fresh and green. Avoid old curry leaves that are dry and stiff.

▶▶ Execution

- Dilute the tamarind paste in 3 cups water and set aside.
- Heat the oil in a casserole pot on high flame for 1 minute.
- Add mustard seeds and allow them to splutter.
- Add cumin seeds and fry for 20-25 seconds.

- Add curry leaves, garlic, and asafoetida. Fry for 1 minute.
- Add tomatoes, tamarind juice, salt, and *rasam* powder.
- Boil on medium flame for 10 minutes or till tomatoes turn soft.

⏩ Testing & Optimization

- If the *rasam* powder does not suffice for spiciness, you can add a few dry red chillies to the seasoning. I have seen *rasam* varieties with green chillies too. In Andhra Pradesh, there is a variety of *rasam* known as *pachchi rasam* which is raw green chillies and onion pieces floating in tamarind juice (the dish is not cooked)

⏩ Suggested Deployment

Rasam is eaten with rice.

CHANA DAL

Spicy Bengal Gram Lentil   Serves 2

High-Level Project Overview

Bengal gram is a more full-bodied *dal* than red gram, with a richer nutty taste. *Chana*, which is essentially split chickpeas, is 25 to 28 per cent protein and can be consumed in a wide variety of ways like *dal*, curry, salad, snacks or ground into flour (i.e. gram flour) and used to make *roti*.

Project Schedule

30 minutes in parallel execution mode

Inventory & Procurement

1 cup / 200 gm Bengal gram (*chana* dal)
1 tsp / 5 gm Turmeric (*haldi*) powder
1 tsp / 5 gm Salt
3 tbsp / 45 ml Vegetable oil
1 tsp / 3 gm Mustard seeds (*rai*)
¼ tsp Asafoetida (*hing*) powder
1 Onion, medium-sized, finely chopped
1 tsp / 6 gm Ginger-garlic (*adrak-lasan*) paste
1 tsp / 5 gm Red chilli powder
1 tsp / 5 gm *Garam masala* powder
2 Tomatoes, medium-sized

Quality Assurance

- Wash *dal*, tomatoes, and peeled onions in running water.
- Wait for cooker to depressurize before opening.

Execution

Subroutine 1 – Cooking the dal (15 minutes)

- Place *dal* in pressure cooker with turmeric powder and salt.
- Add water 1:2 ratio. Pressure cook till 14 whistles.
- Boil some water in a saucepan and add the whole tomatoes. Let the tomatoes remain in the boiling water until the skin begins to split, this usually takes about a minute. Remove the tomatoes immediately, allow cooling and then peel the skin using your fingers. Chop into 8-10 small pieces and set aside.

Subroutine 2 – Preparing the masala (20 minutes)

- Heat the oil in a pan on high flame for 1 minute.
- Add mustard seeds and allow them to splutter.
- Add asafoetida, chopped onions, and ginger-garlic paste and fry for 5 minutes on medium flame.
- Add red chilli powder and *garam masala*. Fry for 30 seconds.
- Add chopped tomatoes, lid the pan and allow cooking for 10 minutes.

Subroutine 3 - Integration (2 minutes)

- Add the *dal* to the *masala*. Mix well and cook for 1 minute.
- Garnish with chopped green coriander leaves.

▸▸ Suggested Deployment

Chana dal can be eaten with *missi roti* (see p. 158) or *sada paratha* (see p. 150) and accompanied with vegetables like *bharwan Shimla mirch* (see p. 119).

DAL MAKHNI

Black Gram Cooked with Kidney Beans Serves 2

High-Level Project Overview

Food of the hardworking Punjabis, this dish packs calories by the truckload and uploads enough energy to toil the fields for a whole day. A rich tasty dish, the lentils provide the protein and the butter and cream provides the energy to work in the fields all day.

▸▸ Project Schedule

45 minutes in parallel execution mode

▸▸ Inventory & Procurement

1 cup / 200 gm Whole black gram (*urad dal*)
¼ cup / 50 gm Kidney beans (*rajma*)
3 tbsp / 50 gm Butter
2 tbsp / 30 ml Vegetable oil
1 tsp / 3 gm Cumin (*jeera*) seeds
2 Onions, medium-sized
2 tsp / 12 gm Ginger-garlic (*adrak-lasan*) paste
1 tsp / 5 gm *Garam masala* powder
1 tsp / 5 gm Turmeric (*haldi*) powder
2 tsp / 10 gm Coriander (*dhaniya*) powder
1 tsp / 5 gm Red chilli powder
2 tsp / 10 gm Salt
3¼ tbsp / 50 ml Cream
½ cup / 30 gm Green coriander (*hara dhaniya*) leaves

▸▸ Quality Assurance

- Wash *dals*, tomatoes, peeled onions and coriander leaves in running water.
- Do not heat butter alone in the pan as it burns easily. Always heat it with some oil.
- Ensure there is thrice the amount of water when soaking lentils overnight. They expand on absorbing water and rise in the vessel, pushing the lentils at the top above the water level if there is just enough water to cover them. Consequently, the lentils above the water level will not soak and remain undercooked in the dish.

- When adding spice powders to the frying onion paste, wait till the water content in the onions has reduced. You want to fry the spices, not boil them.
- Wait for cooker to depressurize before opening.

▸▸ Execution

Subroutine 1 – Preparing dal (20 minutes)

- Soak the *dals* overnight in plenty of water.
- Place the *dals*, 1 tsp salt and water covering up to 3" above the *dal* level in a pressure cooker. Cook till 14 whistles on high flame.
- Take quarter of the *dal* and mash with a masher (if you don't have one, use a fork or a large metal spoon).
- Leave the remaining *dal* in the pressure cooker. Do not strain the excess water. Set aside.

Subroutine 2 – Preparing masala (30 minutes)

- While the *dals* are cooking it would be time saving to start preparing the *masala*. Boil water in a saucepan and add the whole tomatoes. Let the tomatoes remain in the boiling water until the skin begins to split, this usually takes about a minute. Remove the tomatoes immediately, allow cooling and peel the skin using your fingers. Grind the tomatoes into a smooth paste in a blender and set aside.
- Grind the onion into a paste in a blender (do not add water as the onions have enough natural water content inside them) and set aside.
- Heat the butter and oil in a casserole pot on medium flame till butter melts.
- Add cumin seeds and fry for 20-25 seconds.
- Add the onion paste and ginger-garlic paste, fry for 10 minutes till all the water content has evaporated (you will know this when the paste starts to turn brown and sticks to the bottom of the pan).
- Add the *garam masala*, turmeric, coriander and red chilli powders. Fry for 30 seconds.
- Add tomato purée and cook for further 10 minutes, stirring constantly. The longer you leave this *masala* the more concentrated it becomes and emanates more flavours. If you have the time to let it cook longer then turn the flame to a simmer. At this point the *masala* looks deep brown in colour and starts to stick to the pan as all the moisture has evaporated.

Subroutine 3 – Integration (10 minutes)

- Add the *dal*, including the mashed *dal* and some of the water from Subroutine 1 to the *masala* prepared in Subroutine 2.
- Add the remaining 1 tsp salt.
- Mix thoroughly and cook for 10 minutes. At this stage check the consistency and add more water, if desired.
- Switch off flame and add cream.
- Garnish with chopped fresh coriander leaves before serving.

⏩ Testing & Optimization

- You can replace ginger-garlic paste with finely chopped ginger. The ginger pieces create an interesting flavourful experience when chewed.
- You can add some milk instead of water. It will give the dish a more heavy body.

⏩ Suggested Deployment

Dal makhni can be eaten with rice or *rotis* and vegetables like *bhindi fry* (see p. 68) or *bharwan baingan* (see p. 98).

CHANA MASALA

Spicy Chickpeas

Serves 2

> **High-Level Project Overview**
>
> Chickpeas was first domesticated and consumed in Turkey dating as far back as 3500 BC. In India it is commonly found in two varieties, the domestic Indian variety (*kala chana*) and the *kabuli* variety (in this dish we are using the *kabuli* variety). Chickpeas rate among the highest protein content pulses making them an ideal substitute for meat. *Chana masala* is a quintessential North Indian dish great for parties and picnics.

▸▸ Project Schedule

32 minutes in parallel execution mode

▸▸ Inventory & Procurement

2½ cups / 500 gm Chickpeas (*kabuli chana*)
3 tbsp / 45 ml Vegetable oil)
1 tsp / 3 gm Cumin (*jeera*) seeds
2 Onions, medium-sized
3 Green chillies
2 tsp / 12 gm Ginger-garlic (*adrak-lasan*) paste
1 tsp / 5 gm Red chilli powder
2 tsp / 10 gm Coriander (*dhaniya* powder
1 tsp / 5 gm Turmeric (*haldi*) powder
1 tsp / 5 gm *Garam masala* powder
4 Tomatoes, medium-sized
2 tsp / 10 gm Salt
½ cup / 30 gm Green coriander (*hara dhaniya*) leaves

▸▸ Quality Assurance

- Wash tomatoes, green chillies, peeled onions and coriander leaves in running water.
- Sift through chickpeas and remove damaged / blackened / green peas.
- Ensure there is thrice the amount of water when soaking chickpeas overnight. They expand on absorbing water and will rise in the vessel, pushing the chickpeas at the top above the water level if there is just enough water to cover them.

Consequently, these chickpeas outside the water level will not soak further and will remain undercooked in the dish.

- Wait for cooker to depressurize before opening.
- When adding spice powders to the frying onion paste, wait till the water content in the onions has reduced. You want to fry the spices, not boil them.

▸▸ Execution

Subroutine 1 – Preparing chickpeas (20 minutes)

- Soak chickpeas in a large quantity of water overnight. Wash and drain.
- Place chickpeas, 1 tsp salt and water covering up to 3" above chickpea level in a pressure cooker. Cook till 14 whistles on high flame. Eat a few chickpeas at this stage to check, if they are not completely tender in the mouth resume pressure cooking for another 5 whistles. Ensure there is sufficient water before resuming pressure cooking.
- Take out a quarter of the chickpeas into a separate container and mash with a masher (if you don't have one, use a fork or a large metal spoon).
- Leave the remaining chickpeas in the pressure cooker. Do not strain the excess water. Set aside.

Subroutine 2 – Preparing masala (30 minutes)

- While chickpeas are cooking it would be time saving to start preparing the *masala*. Boil water in a saucepan and add the whole tomatoes. Let the tomatoes remain in the boiling water until the skin begins to split, this usually takes about a minute. Remove the tomatoes immediately, allow cooling and peel the skin using your fingers. Grind the tomatoes into a smooth paste in a blender and set aside.
- Grind the onions and green chillies into a paste in a blender (do not add water as the onions have enough natural water content inside them) and set aside.
- Heat the oil in a casserole pot on high flame for 1 minute.
- Add cumin seeds and fry for 20-25 seconds.
- Add the onion-green chilli paste and ginger-garlic paste to the oil, fry for 10 minutes till all the water content has evaporated (you will know this when the paste starts to turn brown and sticks to the bottom of the pan).
- Add red chilli, coriander, turmeric, and *garam masala* powders, and stir well for 30 seconds.

- Add tomato purée and cook for further 10 minutes, stirring constantly. The longer you leave this *masala* the more concentrated it becomes and emanates more flavours. If you have the time to let it cook longer then turn the flame to a simmer. At this point the *masala* looks deep brown in colour and starts to stick to the pan as all the moisture has evaporated.

Subroutine 3 – Integration (10 minutes)

- Add the chickpeas, mashed chickpeas, and some water from Subroutine 1 to the prepared *masala*.
- Add the remaining salt.
- Mix thoroughly and cook for 10 minutes. At this stage, check the consistency and add more water, if desired.
- Garnish with chopped green coriander leaves.

⏩ Testing & Optimization

- You can add juice of 1 lemon to get a tangy taste.
- If the dish appears too watery, mash more chickpeas directly in the pan.

⏩ Suggested Deployment

Chana masala can be eaten with *roti*, *paratha* or *puri* and accompanied with *raita* and onion salad.

RAJMA MASALA

Spicy Kidney Beans in Tomato Gravy

Serves 2

High-Level Project Overview

Rajma is a popular pulse in North India and traces its origins to Latin America. Known in English as red kidney beans due to its colour and kidney shape, *rajma* was traditionally used in dishes that cooked for hours while womenfolk finished other chores such as washing clothes and cleaning front yards. Today it has emblematic significance in cuisines from around the world.

▸▸ Project Schedule

45 minutes in parallel execution mode

▸▸ Inventory & Procurement

2½ cups / 500 gm Kidney beans (*rajma*)
3 tbsp / 45 ml Vegetable oil
1 tsp / 3 gm Cumin (*jeera*) seeds
2 Onions, medium-sized
2 tsp / 12 gm Ginger-garlic (*adrak-lasan*) paste
1 tsp / 5 gm Red chilli powder
2 tsp / 10 gm Coriander (*dhaniya*) powder
1 tsp / 5 gm Turmeric (*haldi*) powder
1 tsp / 5 gm *Garam masala* powder
4 Tomatoes, medium-sized
2 tsp / 10 gm Salt
½ cup / 30 gm Green coriander (*hara dhaniya*) leaves

▸▸ Quality Assurance

- Wash tomatoes, red chillies, green coriander leaves, and peeled onions in running water.
- Sift through the kidney beans and remove the damaged ones.
- Ensure there is thrice the amount of water when soaking kidney beans overnight. They expand on absorbing water and will rise in the vessel, pushing the beans at the top above the water level if there is just enough water to cover them. Consequently, these beans outside the water level will not soak further and remain undercooked in the dish.
- Wait for cooker to depressurize before opening.

- When adding spice powders to the frying onion paste, wait till the water content in the onions has reduced. You want to fry the spices, not boil them.

▶▶ Execution

Subroutine 1 – Preparing kidney beans (20 minutes)

- Soak kidney beans overnight in a large quantity of water. Wash and drain.
- Place the beans with 1 tsp salt and water covering up to 3" above kidney beans level in a pressure cooker. Cook till 14 whistles on high flame.
- Eat a few beans at this stage to check, if they are not completely tender in the mouth resume pressure cooking till another 5 whistles. Ensure there is sufficient water before resuming pressure cooking.
- Take out a quarter of the beans into a separate container and mash with a masher (if you don't have one, use a fork or a large metal spoon).
- Leave the remaining kidney beans in the pressure cooker. Do not strain the excess water. Set aside.

Subroutine 2 – Preparing masala (30 minutes)

- While kidney beans are cooking it would be time saving to start preparing the *masala*. Boil water in a saucepan and add the whole tomatoes. Let the tomatoes remain in the boiling water until the skin begins to split, this usually takes about a minute. Remove the tomatoes immediately, allow cooling and peel the skin using your fingers. Grind the tomatoes into a smooth paste in a blender and set aside.
- Grind the onions into a paste in a blender (do not add water as the onions have enough natural water content inside them) and set aside.
- Slit the red chillies lengthwise and set aside.
- Heat the oil in a casserole pot on high flame for 1 minute.
- Add cumin seeds and fry for 20-25 seconds.
- Add the onion paste and ginger-garlic paste, fry for 10 minutes till all the water content has evaporated (you will know this when the paste starts to turn brown and sticks to the bottom of the pan).
- Add red chilli, coriander, turmeric and *garam masala* powders, and stir well for 30 seconds.
- Add tomato purée and cook for further 10 minutes, stirring constantly. The longer you leave this *masala* the more concentrated it becomes and emanates more flavours. If you have the time to let it cook longer then turn the flame to simmer.

At this point the *masala* looks deep brown in colour and starts to stick to the pan as all the moisture has evaporated.

Subroutine 3 – Integration (10 minutes)

- Add the boiled kidney beans, mashed kidney beans and some of the water from Subroutine 1 to the *masala* prepared in Subroutine 2.
- Add 1 tsp salt.
- Mix thoroughly and cook for 10 minutes. At this stage check the consistency and add more water, if desired.
- Garnish with chopped green coriander leaves.

▸▸ Testing & Optimization

- If the dish appears too watery, mash more kidney beans directly in the pan.

▸▸ Suggested Deployment

Rajma masala can be eaten with rice or *roti* and accompanied with vegetables like *jhatpat paneer* (see p. 74) or *bhein mazedaar* (see p. 86).

LOBIYA MASALA

Spicy Black-eyed Beans

Serves 2

High-Level Project Overview

The black-eyed bean is a popular bean originally cultivated in Asia and Africa. An excellent source of calcium and vitamin A, it is the staple food in many parts of the world as it grows well in hardy climates. In West Africa, where I spent most of my childhood, black-eyed beans were called local beans and were used to make *kosé* (large deep-fried *pakoras* made of soaked and ground beans, eaten with bread and a dip made of unrefined palm oil mixed with red chilli powder and salt).

▸▸ Project Schedule

45 minutes in parallel execution mode

▸▸ Inventory & Procurement

500 gm Black-eyed beans (*lobiya*), large
2 tsp / 10 gm Salt
3 tbsp / 45 ml Vegetable oil
1 tsp / 3 gm Cumin (*jeera*) seeds
2 Onions, medium-sized
2 tsp / 12 gm Ginger-garlic (*adrak-lasan*) paste
3 Green chillies
1 tsp / 5 gm Red chilli powder
2 tsp / 10 gm Coriander (*dhaniya*) powder
1 tsp / 5 gm Turmeric (*haldi*) powder
1 tsp / 5 gm *Garam masala* powder
4 Tomatoes, medium-sized
3" piece Ginger

▸▸ Quality Assurance

- Scrape ginger with a knife to remove skin.
- Wash ginger, tomatoes, and peeled onions in running water.
- Sift through beans and remove the damaged ones.
- Ensure there is thrice the amount of water when soaking beans overnight. They expand on absorbing water and will rise in the vessel, pushing the beans at the top above the water level if there is just enough water to cover them. Consequently,

these beans outside the water level will not soak further and remain undercooked in the dish.

- Wait for cooker to depressurize before opening.
- When adding spice powders to the frying onion paste, wait till the water content in the onions has reduced. You want to fry the spices, not boil them.

▸▸ Execution

Subroutine 1 – Preparing beans (20 minutes)

- Soak beans in a large quantity of water overnight. Wash and drain.
- Place beans with 1 tsp salt and water covering up to 3" above beans level in a pressure cooker. Cook till 14 whistles on high flame.
- Eat a few beans at this stage to check, if they are not completely tender in the mouth resume pressure cooking till another 5 whistles. Ensure there is sufficient water before resuming pressure cooking.
- Take out a quarter of the beans into a separate container and mash with a masher (if you don't have one, use a fork or a large metal spoon).
- Leave the remaining beans in the pressure cooker. Do not strain the excess water. Set aside.

Subroutine 2 – Preparing masala (30 minutes)

- While beans are cooking it would be time saving to start preparing the *masala*. Boil water in a saucepan and add the whole tomatoes. Let the tomatoes remain in the boiling water until the skin begins to split, this usually takes about a minute. Remove the tomatoes immediately, allow cooling and peel the skin using your fingers. Grind the tomatoes into a smooth paste in a blender and set aside.
- Grind the onions into a paste in a blender (do not add water as the onions have enough natural water content inside them) and set aside.
- Slice ginger and green chillies into thin strips, set aside.
- Heat the oil in a casserole pot on high flame for 1 minute.
- Add cumin seeds and fry for 20-25 seconds.
- Add onion paste and ginger-garlic paste to the oil, fry for 10 minutes till all the water content has evaporated (you will know this when the paste starts to turn brown and sticks to the bottom of the pan).
- Add red chilli, coriander, turmeric and *garam masala* powders and stir well for 30 seconds.

- Add tomato purée and cook for further 10 minutes, stirring constantly. The longer you leave this *masala* the more concentrated it becomes and emanates more flavours. If you have the time to let it cook longer then turn the flame to simmer. At this point the *masala* looks deep brown in colour and starts to stick to the pan as all the moisture has evaporated.

Subroutine 3 – Integration (10 minutes)

- Add the boiled beans, mashed beans and some of the water from Subroutine 1 to the *masala* prepared in Subroutine 2.
- Add 1 tsp salt.
- Mix thoroughly and cook for 10 minutes. At this stage check the consistency and add more water, if desired.
- Garnish with ginger and green chilli strips before serving.

▸▸ Testing & Optimization

- You can add the juice of 1 lemon to get a tangy taste
- If the dish appears too watery, mash more beans directly in the pan

▸▸ Suggested Deployment

Lobiya masala can be eaten with rice or *missi roti* (see p. 158) and accompanied with vegetables like *kurkuri arvi* (see p. 76), *bhein mazedaar* (see p. 86) or *masaledaar kaccha kela* (see p. 84).

VEGETABLE KOFTA

Vegetable Dumplings in Creamy Gravy

Serves 4

> **High-Level Project Overview**
>
> With Persian roots, the *kofta* was originally balls of lamb or beef meat mixed with spices, cooked and served in gravy. As travellers took this dish to lands they immigrated to, it took various forms by imbibing the traditions of the local cuisines. In India where vegetarianism is popular, *koftas* are often made with vegetables, deep-fried and served immersed in thick, spicy gravy.

▸▸ Project Schedule

45 minutes in parallel execution mode

▸▸ Inventory & Procurement

For the koftas

3 Carrots (*gajar*), medium-sized

250 gm Cabbage (*bandh gobi*)

2 Green chillies

4 tbsp / 40 gm Gram flour (*besan*)

1 tsp / 5 gm Salt

2½ cups / 500 ml Vegetable oil

For the gravy

3 tbsp / 45 ml Vegetable oil

1 tsp / 3 gm Cumin (*jeera*) seeds

4 Cloves (*laung*)

1 Bay leaf (*tej patta*), large

2 tsp / 12 gm Ginger-garlic (*adrak-lasan*) paste

½ tsp / 2½ gm Asafoetida (*hing*) powder

1 tsp / 5 gm *Garam masala* powder

1 tsp / 5 gm Red chilli powder

1 tsp / 5 gm Turmeric (*haldi*) powder

6 Tomatoes, large

1 tsp / 5 gm Salt

2½ tbsp / 50 ml Cream

½ cup / 30 gm Green coriander (*hara dhaniya*) leaves

▸▸ Quality Assurance

- Peel and wash carrots in running water.
- Remove the outer layer of the cabbage and wash in running water.
- Wash tomatoes, green chillies, and coriander leaves in running water.
- Do not heat the dish after adding cream as this will cause the cream to curdle.

▶▶ Execution

Subroutine 1 – Preparing koftas (30 minutes)

- Finely chop the green chillies and set aside.
- Grate the carrots and cabbage in a blender using the grating blade (if you don't have a multi-purpose blender, then use a manual grater).
- Put the grated carrot and cabbage in a bowl, add 1 tsp salt. Mix and set aside for 5 minutes.
- Take a palm-full of mixture and squeeze out the water. Repeat this process for the entire mixture.
- Add the green chillies and gram flour. Knead well till all the ingredients are thoroughly mixed (if the mix is still wet, keep adding more gram flour till all the water is absorbed).
- Take a small amount of the mixture in your hand and roll into a ball of 2" diameter. Repeat this process for the entire mixture. You should get approx.imately 15 balls when done.
- Heat 2½ cups of oil in a frying pan for 2 minutes on high flame.
- Reduce flame to medium and add half the vegetable balls; fry till they are golden brown (turn them over in the oil so all sides cook evenly). Remove the balls and place on clean paper towel to soak excess oil.
- Repeat for the remaining vegetable balls.

Subroutine 2 – Preparing masala (15 minutes)

- Boil water in a saucepan and add the whole tomatoes. Let the tomatoes remain in the boiling water until the skin begins to split, this usually takes about a minute. Remove the tomatoes immediately, allow cooling and then peel the skin using your fingers. Blend the tomatoes in a blender.
- Heat the oil in a casserole pot on high flame for 1 minute.
- Add cumin seeds, cloves, and bay leaf. Fry for 20-25 seconds.
- Add ginger-garlic paste, asafoetida, *garam masala*, turmeric and red chilli powders. Fry for 30 seconds.
- Add the tomato purée and salt, lid the pan and cook for further 15 minutes, stirring constantly.

Subroutine 3 – Integration (20 minutes)

- Add 2 cups water to the tomato *masala* and bring to the boil on high flame.
- Turn off the heat. Carefully add the koftas from Subroutine 1 to the gravy making sure they are all submerged. Lid the pan and leave to soak for 10 minutes.

- Pour cream into the dish in a spiral pattern and sprinkle chopped green coriander leaves before serving.

▸▸ Testing & Optimization

- You can experiment with the gravy by adding one onion blended or chopped finely.
- You can lend a rich taste to the dish by replacing oil with ghee.
- You can replace some cream in Subroutine 3 with milk if you want thicker gravy.

▸▸ Suggested Deployment

Vegetable kofta can be eaten with rice, *mooli paratha* (see p. 154) and dry fried vegetables like *bharwan baingan* (see p. 98) or *bharwan bhindi* (see p. 82).

PALAK PANEER

Cottage Cheese in Spinach Gravy

Serves 2

High-Level Project Overview

Introduced by Persian and Turkish migrants (Central and Eurasian republics such as Azerbaijan and Kazakhstan), cottage cheese (*paneer*) is the dominantly consumed type of cheese in India. It's quick and easy-to-make at home, unlike western cheeses which require professional skills. *Palak Paneer* is a popular dish in North India prepared with puréed spinach. This dish has infinite variations making it an obvious choice for home-keepers who need to experiment constantly to keep palate and family happy.

▸▸ Project Schedule

35 minutes in parallel execution mode

▸▸ Inventory & Procurement

5 bundles Spinach (*palak*)
200 gm Cottage cheese (*paneer*)
3 tbsp / 45 ml Vegetable oil
1 tsp / 3 gm Cumin (*jeera*) seeds
1 Onion, large
2 Green chillies
2 tsp / 12 gm Ginger-garlic (*adrak-lasan*) paste
1 tsp / 5 gm *Garam masala* powder
1 tsp / 5 gm Turmeric (*haldi*) powder
2 tsp / 10 gm Coriander (*dhaniya*) powder
2 Tomatoes, large
2 tsp / 10 gm Salt
1 tbsp / 15 ml Cream

▸▸ Quality Assurance

- Snip spinach leaves from stalks and wash thoroughly in running water.
- Wash tomatoes, peeled onion, and green chillies in running water.
- Unless you like everything absolutely fresh and homemade, you can buy frozen cottage cheese from the local supermarket.
- When adding spice powders to the frying onion paste, wait till the water content in the onion has reduced. You want to fry the spices, not boil them.

▸▸ Execution

Subroutine 1 – Preparing spinach purée (20 minutes)

- Bring some water to the boil in a casserole pan and switch the flame off.
- Add spinach to boiled water and place lid. Keep spinach in this for 10 minutes.
- Grind the blanched spinach in a blender. Set aside.

Subroutine 2 – Preparing masala (30 minutes)

- Boil water in a saucepan and add the whole tomatoes. Let the tomatoes remain in boiling water until the skin begins to split (about 1 minute). Remove immediately, cool and peel the skin using fingers. Blend tomatoes in a blender. Set aside.
- Grind onion and green chillies into a paste in the blender (do not add water as the onions have enough natural water content inside them).
- Heat the oil in a casserole pot on high flame for 1 minute.
- Add cumin seeds and fry for 20-25 seconds.
- Add the onion-green chilli and ginger-garlic pastes to the oil, fry for 10 minutes on medium flame till all the water content has evaporated (you will know this when the paste starts to turn brown and sticks to the bottom of the pan).
- Add the *garam masala*, turmeric, and coriander powders and salt. Fry for 30 seconds.
- Add tomato purée and cook for further 10 minutes, stirring constantly.

Subroutine 3 – Integration (10 minutes)

- Cut cottage cheese into 1" cubes (if not already purchased that way).
- Add the spinach purée and cottage cheese cubes to the *masala* prepared in Subroutine 2. Cook for 10 minutes and switch flame off.
- Garnish by pouring cream into the dish in a spiral pattern before serving.

▸▸ Testing & Optimization

- Cottage cheese can be replaced with a variety of substitutes like boiled potato cubes, gram flour koftas, boiled chickpeas, etc.
- You can replace ginger-garlic paste with thin ginger slices.
- You can replace the cream garnish with a blob of butter.

▸▸ Suggested Deployment

Palak paneer can be eaten with rice or *missi roti* (see p. 158).

BHEIN AUR ALOO MASALA

Sautéed Lotus Stem and Potato

Serves 4

High-Level Project Overview

The lotus plant enjoys tremendous religious significance in India, with the lotus flower being India's national flower and the preferred throne of the goddess of wealth, Mahalakshmi. The lotus flower also signifies purity, prosperity and fertility in East Asian cultures. The entire plant is edible with various parts used to make everything from soothing potions to jams and curries.

⏩ Project Schedule

30 minutes in linear execution mode

⏩ Inventory & Procurement

2 Lotus stems (*bhein*), medium-sized
2 Potatoes, medium-sized
3 tbsp / 45 ml Vegetable oil
1 tsp / 3 gm Cumin (*jeera*) seeds
1 tsp / 5 gm *Garam masala* powder
1 tsp / 5 gm Turmeric (*haldi*) powder
1 tsp / 5 gm Red chilli powder
2 tsp / 10 gm Salt
6 Tomatoes, medium-sized
1 tsp / 5 gm Mango powder (*amchur*)
2 tbsp / 8 gm Green coriander (*hara dhaniya*) leaves

⏩ Quality Assurance

- Wash lotus stems, tomatoes, and potatoes in running water.
- Keep chopped potato pieces in salt water to prevent oxidation.

⏩ Execution

- Cut the lotus stem into ¼" slices.
- Peel and cut the potatoes into ¼" pieces
- Boil water in a saucepan and add the whole tomatoes. Let the tomatoes remain in the boiling water until the skin begins to split, this usually takes about a minute. Remove the tomatoes immediately, allow cooling and then peel the skin using your fingers. Chop each tomato into 8-10 small pieces.

- Heat the oil in a casserole pot on high flame for 1 minute.
- Add cumin seeds and fry for 20-25 seconds. Reduce flame to medium.
- Add *garam masala*, turmeric and red chilli powders, and salt. Fry for 30 seconds.
- Add the chopped tomatoes, lid the pan and cook for further 10 minutes stirring constantly till tomato becomes a paste.
- Add the lotus stem and potato pieces to the *masala* and cook for 5 minutes allowing the pieces to absorb the *masala* flavours.
- Add 2 cups of water, or enough to cover the vegetables, and bring to the boil on high flame.
- Once the gravy starts to boil, reduce flame to medium and simmer for 20 minutes.
- Add the mango powder before switching the flame off.
- Garnish with fresh chopped coriander.

▸▸ Testing & Optimization

- You can replace mango powder with juice of one lemon.

▸▸ Suggested Deployment

This preparation can be eaten with rice or *roti* accompanied with *Shimla mirch raita* (see p. 164).

ANDA MASALA

Eggs in Aromatic Gravy

Serves 4

High-Level Project Overview

Egg *masala* is boiled eggs served in flavourful gravy. Popular in the 'Irani' chai cafes of Hyderabad, this dish is a favourite among busy hungry road-warriors needing quick and nutritious food in the Hyderabadi tropical heat.

▸▸ Project Schedule

30 minutes in parallel execution mode

▸▸ Inventory & Procurement

8 Eggs
2 Onions, medium-sized
2 Green chillies
1 cup Fenugreek (*methi*) leaves
4 Tomatoes, medium-sized
3 tbsp / 45 ml Vegetable oil
1 tsp / 3 gm Cumin (*jeera*) seeds
6 Cloves (*laung*)
1 Bay leaf (*tej patta*), large
2 tsp / 12 gm Ginger-garlic (*adrak-lasan*) paste
1 tsp / 5 gm *Garam masala* powder
1 tsp / 5 gm Turmeric (*haldi*) powder
1 tsp / 5 gm Red chilli powder
2 tsp / 10 gm Coriander (*dhaniya*) powder
2 tsp / 10 gm Salt

▸▸ Quality Assurance

- Always place eggs in cold water before starting the flame. This will prevent the eggs from breaking if added directly into hot water.
- Wash tomatoes, peeled onions, and green chillies in running water.
- When adding spice powders to the frying onion paste, wait till the water content in the onions has reduced. You want to fry the spices, not boil them.

▸▸ Execution

Subroutine 1 – Preparing eggs (10 minutes)

- Place eggs into a saucepan, add enough water to cover the eggs and bring the water to the boil on high flame.
- Reduce flame to medium and simmer for 8 minutes.

- Drain the water from the pan and add cold water.
- Crack the egg shells with the back of a spoon or on your work surface and remove shell completely. Set aside.

Subroutine 2 – Preparing masala (30 minutes)

- Grind the onions, green chillies, and fenugreek leaves into a paste in a blender (do not add water as onions have enough natural water content inside them). Set aside.
- Boil water in a saucepan and add the whole tomatoes. Let the tomatoes remain in the boiling water until the skin begins to split, this usually takes about a minute. Remove the tomatoes immediately, allow cooling and then peel the skin using your fingers. Grind the tomatoes in the blender and set aside (tomato purée).
- Heat the oil in a casserole pot on high flame for 1 minute.
- Add cumin seeds, cloves, and bay leaf. Fry for 30 seconds.
- Add the onion-green chilli-fenugreek paste and ginger-garlic paste to the oil and fry for 10 minutes on medium flame till all the water content has evaporated (you will know this when the paste starts to turn brown and sticks to the bottom of the pan).
- Add the *garam masala*, turmeric, red chilli, and coriander powders, and salt. Fry for 30 seconds.
- Add the tomato purée and cook for further 10 minutes, stirring constantly.
- Add 1 cup water to make thick gravy.

Subroutine 3 – integration (3 minutes)

- Add the eggs to the *masala*. Cook for 3 minutes.

▸▸ Testing & Optimization

- You can cut the eggs into halves before adding to gravy as this allows the gravy to penetrate the eggs.
- You can shallow-fry the eggs before adding them to the *masala*.

▸▸ Suggested Deployment

Anda masala can be eaten with rice or *rotis*.

GUCCHI MATAR KI SUBZI

Spicy Mushroom and Pea Curry

Serves 4

High-Level Project Overview

Edible mushrooms were first cultivated in India back in the 1950s in Himachal Pradesh. The most popular variety grown, consumed and exported is the white button mushrooms. Mushrooms are fat-free and a great source of proteins, vitamin C and iron, making them a perfect choice for the sedentary IT worker.

▸▸ Project Schedule

30 minutes in linear execution mode

▸▸ Inventory & Procurement

500 gm Mushrooms (*gucchi*)
200 gm Green peas (*hara matar*)
3 tbsp / 45 ml Vegetable oil
1 tsp / 3 gm Cumin (*jeera*) seeds
2 tsp / 10 gm *Tandoori masala*
1 tsp / 5 gm Turmeric (*haldi*) powder
1 tsp / 5 gm Red chilli powder
2 tsp / 10 gm Salt
6 Tomatoes

▸▸ Quality Assurance

- When shopping for mushrooms, select the whitest ones with firm texture.
- Mushrooms sitting on supermarket shelves for too long will have brown or black discolourations.

▸▸ Execution

- Cut the mushrooms into 4 slices each.
- If using fresh peas, extract from the pod and set aside.
- Boil water in a saucepan and add the whole tomatoes. Let the tomatoes remain in the boiling water until the skin begins to split. This usually takes about a minute. Remove the tomatoes immediately, allow cooling and then peel skin using your fingers. Chop each tomato into 8-10 small pieces.
- Heat the oil in a pan on high flame for 1 minute.

- Add cumin seeds and fry for 20-25 seconds.
- Add the *tandoori masala*, turmeric and red chilli powders, and salt. Fry for 30 seconds.
- Add the chopped tomatoes, lid the pan and cook for further 10 minutes, stirring constantly until the tomatoes become paste-like.
- Add the mushrooms and peas with 1 cup water, cook on medium flame for 15 minutes. Add more water, if necessary.

▸▸ Testing & Optimization

- You can add some chopped onions if you desire.
- You can thicken the gravy by using cashew nut powder paste or yoghurt.

▸▸ Suggested Deployment

This dish can be eaten with *parathas*.

ARVI TAMATAR MASALA

Colocasia in Tomato Gravy

Serves 4

High-Level Project Overview

Consumed in India and dating as long back as 5000 BC, *arvi*, known in English as colocasia, is the boorish hairy country cousin of the aristocratic potato. It does not, however, carry the neutral taste of potato as its higher protein content gives it a rather meat-like taste. Once considered the ideal food for slaves, *arvi* today has venerable position in Indian cuisine for its rich earthy flavour.

▸▸ Project Schedule

30 minutes in parallel execution mode

▸▸ Inventory & Procurement

500 gm Colocasia (*arvi*), fresh
6 Tomatoes, medium-sized
2 Onions, medium-sized
2 Green chillies
3 tbsp / 45 ml Vegetable oil
1 tsp / 3 m Carom seeds (*ajwain*)
3" piece Ginger (*adrak*)
¼ tsp Asafoetida (*hing*) powder
1 tsp / 5 gm Red chilli powder
1 tsp / 5 gm Turmeric (*haldi*) powder
2 tsp / 10 gm Salt
2 tsp / 6 gm Cumin (*jeera*) seeds
½ cup / 30 gm Green coriander (*hara dhaniya*) leaves

▸▸ Quality Assurance

- Scrape ginger with a knife to remove skin before chopping into pieces.
- When shopping for colocasia, select tubers with rich waxy look. Colocasia sitting on the shelves for too long will have a dry look and the packet will have debris inside, this debris is the skin falling off due to dryness.
- Wash ginger, green coriander leaves, colocasia, peeled onions, and tomatoes in running water.
- Wait for cooker to depressurize before opening.
- When adding spice powders to the frying onion paste, wait till the water content in the onions has reduced. You want to fry the spices, not boil them.

▶▶ Execution

Subroutine 1 – Preparing colocasia (15)

- Cut the colocasia into approx.imately 2" pieces, leaving the skin on.
- Place pieces in pressure cooker with 1 tsp salt and enough water to cover; pressure cook till 2 whistles.
- Drain the colocasia from the water and peel the skin using your fingers. The skin should peel off easily. If you can do this while the colocasia is still warm then peeling is easier. Once it gets cold the skin becomes sticky so peeling is more difficult and time consuming.
- Cut the peeled colocasia into 1" pieces. Set aside.

Subroutine 2 – Preparing masala (30 minutes)

- Chop the ginger and green coriander leaves separately, set aside.
- Roast cumin seeds in a dry pan on high flame for 2 minutes. Powder the roasted seeds in a mortar (if you do not have a mortar-pestle set, place the roasted seeds on a tissue or paper, fold and press over with a rolling pin several times till cumin become powder). Set aside.
- Boil water in a saucepan and add the whole tomatoes. Let the tomatoes remain in the boiling water until the skin begins to split. This usually takes about 1 minute. Remove the tomatoes immediately, allow cooling and then peel skin using your fingers. Chop each tomato into 8-10 small pieces. Set aside.
- Grind the onions and green chillies into a paste in a blender (do not add water as the onions have enough natural water content inside them).
- Heat the oil in a casserole pot on high flame for 1 minute.
- Add carom seeds and fry for 20-25 seconds.
- Add the onion-green chilli paste and ginger pieces to the oil and fry for 10 minutes on medium flame till all the water content has evaporated (you will know this when the paste starts to turn brown and sticks to the bottom of the pan).
- Add the asafoetida, red chilli powder, turmeric powder, and salt. Fry for 30 seconds.
- Add the tomato pieces and cook for further 10 minutes, stirring constantly till the tomatoes become paste-like.

Subroutine 3 – Integration (15 minutes)

- Add the colocasia from Subroutine 1 to the *masala* along with 1 cup water. Place lid and cook on medium flame for 10 minutes.

- Add the roasted cumin powder before switching the flame off.
- Garnish with chopped green coriander leaves before serving.

▸▸ Suggested Deployment

Arvi tamatar masala can be eaten with rice or *roti* accompanied with *dahi lauki* (see p. 121).

PANEER BUTTER MASALA

Creamy Cottage Cheese

Serves 4

High-Level Project Overview

Popular in North India, this dish uses cottage cheese steeped in homemade butter and fragrant spices. It has been customized to suit regional palates – in Punjab it is quite gravy intensive whereas down South it is served more like a vegetable.

▸▸ Project Schedule

45 minutes in parallel execution mode

▸▸ Inventory & Procurement

400 gm Cottage cheese (*paneer*)
4 Tomatoes, medium-sized
2 Onions, medium-sized
2 Green chillies
2 tbsp / 30 ml Vegetable oil
2 tbsp / 30 gm Butter (substitute with gheee if you don't have butter)
1 tsp / 3 gm Cumin (*jeera*) seeds
1 tsp / 6 gm Ginger-garlic (*adrak-lasan*) paste
1 tsp / 5 gm *Garam masala* powder
1 tsp / 5 gm Turmeric (*haldi*) powder
1 tsp / 5 gm Red chilli powder
2 tsp / 10 gm Coriander (*dhaniya*) powder
2 tsp / 10 gm Salt
2 tsp / 10 gm *Tandoori masala*
100 ml Cream, fresh
½ cup / 30 gm Green coriander (*hara dhaniya*) leaves

▸▸ Quality Assurance

- Wash tomatoes, green chillies, green coriander leaves, and peeled onions in running water.
- Unless you prefer using homemade cottage cheese, you can buy the frozen variety from the local supermarket. I use the frozen one that have no preservatives like vinegar in the packing. Ensure to defrost frozen cottage cheese before using.
- The addition of oil to the butter will prevent the butter from burning.
- When adding spice powders to the frying onion paste, wait till the water content in the onions has reduced. You want to fry the spices, not boil them.

▸▸ Execution

Subroutine 1 – Preparing butter masala (30 minutes)

- Boil water in a saucepan and add the whole tomatoes. Let the tomatoes remain in the boiling water until the skin begins to split, this usually takes about a minute. Remove the tomatoes immediately, allow cooling and then peel the skin using your fingers. Grind the tomatoes in the blender and set aside (tomato purée).
- Grind the onions and green chillies into a paste in a blender (do not add water as the onions have enough natural water content inside them).
- In a casserole pot add the butter and oil, heat on medium flame for 1 minute.
- Add cumin seeds and fry for 20-25 seconds.
- Add the onion-green chilli and ginger-garlic pastes and fry for 10 minutes on medium flame till all the water content has evaporated (you will know this when the paste starts to turn brown and sticks to the bottom of the pan).
- Add *garam masala*, turmeric, red chilli and coriander powders, and salt. Fry for 30 seconds.
- Add the tomato purée and cook for further 10 minutes, stirring constantly.

Subroutine 2 – Preparing cottage cheese (5 minutes)

- Cut cottage cheese into 1" cubes (if not already purchased that way).
- Heat some oil in a pan and shallow-fry the cottage cheese cubes for about 5 minutes on medium flame until the sides turn golden brown colour.
- Remove the cubes from the pan and place on a plate lined with a clean paper towel to absorb the excess oil.

Subroutine 3 – Integration (15 minutes)

- Add the fried cottage cheese, *tandoori masala* and 2 cups water to the *masala* and bring to the boil.
- Reduce flame to medium, lid the pan and simmer for 10 minutes. Switch off.
- Garnish with fresh cream and chopped green coriander leaves before serving.

▸▸ Testing & Optimization

- You can experiment by adding more spices such as ground cardamom, cinnamon powder or bay leaf.

▸▸ Suggested Deployment

Paneer butter masala can be eaten with *roti*, *paratha* or rice accompanied with *dum aloo* (see p.108) or *bharwan baingan kishti* (see p. 113).

VADIA AUR ALOO RASEDAAR

Sun-dried Dumplings and Potato Curry Serves 4

High-Level Project Overview

Vadia are spices, herbs, lentils and wet ingredients mixed and dried in the summer sun for several days until they lose their moisture. They are then stored in airtight containers. *Vadias* are deep-fried in oil to be eaten with a meal (South Indian way) or added to vegetables and curries (North Indian way). As the permutations and combinations of spices, lentils and other ingredients are infinite, you will find a mind-boggling variety of *vadias* in the market.

▸▸ Project Schedule

30 minutes in parallel execution mode

▸▸ Inventory & Procurement

1 cup *Vadia*
2 Potatoes, medium-sized
4 Tomatoes, medium-sized
4 tbsp / 60 ml Vegetable oil
1 tsp / 3 gm Cumin (*jeera*) seeds
½ tsp / 2½ gm Asafoetida (*hing*) powder
1 tsp / 5 gm *Garam masala* powder
1 tsp / 5 gm Turmeric (*haldi*) powder
1 tsp / 5 gm Red chilli powder
2 tsp / 10 gm Salt
½ cup / 30 gm Green coriander (*hara dhaniya*) leaves

▸▸ Quality Assurance

- The best place to find *vadia* used to be the aluminium can on the top shelf of your grandma's kitchen (of course, subject to conditions). However, nowadays you will find ready-made *vadia* in most supermarkets. Buy packets that have the least powder at the bottom, if there is much powder in the packaging the *vadias* are probably falling apart from age or have been poorly handled.
- Wash potatoes, tomatoes, and green coriander leaves in running water.
- Wait for cooker to depressurize before opening.

▸▸ Execution

Subroutine 1 – Preparing potatoes (10 minutes)

- Place potatoes with skin in pressure cooker with 1 tsp salt and enough water to cover. Pressure cook till 3 whistles. Remove potatoes, peel skin and cut into medium-sized pieces. Set aside.

Subroutine 2 – Preparing the vadia *masala (15 minutes)*

- Boil water in a saucepan and add the whole tomatoes. Let the tomatoes remain in the boiling water until the skin begins to split. This usually takes about 1 minute. Remove the tomatoes immediately, allow cooling and then peel skin using your fingers. Chop each tomato into 8-10 small pieces. Set aside.
- Heat the oil in a casserole pot on high flame for 1 minute.
- Add cumin seeds and fry for 20-25 seconds.
- Add *vadia* and fry on medium flame for 3 minutes, stirring frequently. The *vadia* should turn a healthy golden brown colour.
- Lower flame and using a spoon, remove half the oil.
- Add asafoetida, *garam masala*, turmeric and red chilli powders and salt; fry for 30 seconds.
- Add chopped tomatoes, lid the pan and cook for further 10 minutes, stirring constantly.

Subroutine 3 – Integration (15 minutes)

- Add potatoes and 4 cups water and bring to the boil on high flame. When gravy starts to boil, reduce flame to medium and simmer for 10 minutes.
- Garnish with chopped green coriander leaves before serving.

▸▸ Testing & Optimization

- You can add 1 tsp tamarind paste to get a tangy taste.

▸▸ Suggested Deployment

This dish can be eaten with *roti* or *paratha* and *raita*. As the *vadias* have an intense character, I do not recommend serving it with equally pungent dishes such as *sambar* or *vangi baht*.

MATAR PANEER

Peas with Cottage Cheese — Serves 4

> **High-Level Project Overview**
>
> *Paneer* is a versatile ingredient for its soft texture and tendency to absorb flavours very well, consequently it can be added to many curries and dry dishes to bring in that little extra flavour. *Matar paneer* is a dish of peas and cottage cheese in a delightfully light curry which can be enjoyed with Indian breads or plain rice. This dish is a ubiquitous part of North Indian *thalis*.

▸▸ Project Schedule

30 minutes in linear execution mode

▸▸ Inventory & Procurement

200 gm Green peas (*hara matar*)
200 gm Cottage cheese (*paneer*)
3 Tomatoes, large
1 Onion, large
2 Green chillies
3 tbsp / 45 ml Vegetable oil
1 tsp / 5 gm Cumin *(jeera)* seeds
2 tsp / 12 gm Ginger-garlic (*adrak-lasan*) paste
1 tsp / 5 gm *Garam masala* powder
1 tsp / 5 gm Turmeric (*haldi*) powder
2 tsp / 10 gm Coriander (*dhaniya*) powder
2 tsp / 10 gm Salt

▸▸ Quality Assurance

- If you have purchased frozen peas, take them out of the freezer well in advance so that they can defrost.
- Wash tomatoes, peeled onion, and green chillies in running water.
- Unless you like everything absolutely fresh and homemade, you can buy frozen cottage cheese from the local supermarket. I use frozen cottage cheese packets since they have no preservatives like vinegar. Ensure to defrost frozen cottage cheese before using.
- Wait for cooker to depressurize before opening.
- When adding spice powders to the frying onion paste, wait till the water content in the onions has reduced. You want to fry the spices, not boil them.

▸▸ Execution

- Boil water in a saucepan and add the whole tomatoes. Let the tomatoes remain in the boiling water until the skin begins to split, this usually takes about a minute. Remove the tomatoes immediately, allow cooling and then peel the skin using your fingers. Grind the tomatoes in the blender and set aside (tomato purée).
- Grind the onion and green chillies into a paste in a blender (do not add water as the onions have enough natural water content inside them).
- Heat the oil on high flame for 1 minute in a pressure cooker.
- Add cumin seeds and fry for 20-25 seconds.
- Add the onion-green chilli and ginger-garlic pastes to the oil, fry for 10 minutes on medium flame till all the water content has evaporated (you will know this when the paste starts to turn brown and sticks to the bottom of the pan).
- Add the *garam masala*, turmeric and coriander powders, and salt. Fry for 30 seconds.
- Add tomato purée, peas and 2 cups water. Place pressure cooker lid and cook till 2 whistles.
- Once cooked add the cottage cheese cubes and simmer for 2 minutes.

▸▸ Testing & Optimization

- You can shallow-fry the cottage cheese cubes before adding then to the peas and *masala*.

▸▸ Suggested Deployment

Matar paneer can be eaten with rice or *rotis* and *parathas*.

ALOO MATAR RASEDAAR

Potato and Pea Curry Serves 2

High-Level Project Overview

The pea-and-potato combination is popular worldwide, with the Europeans eating them with pies and the Irish making them into cream soups. Mashed potatoes with a side order of boiled peas are popularly eaten with steaks in the US. In North India, this combination is known by its Hindi name *aloo matar* and is a ubiquitous dish in *thalis*.

▸▸ Project Schedule

20 minutes in parallel execution mode

▸▸ Inventory & Procurement

200 gm Green peas (*hara matar*)
3 Potatoes, medium-sized
3 Tomatoes, medium-sized
3 tbsp / 45 ml Vegetable oil
1 tsp / 3 gm Cumin (*jeera*) seeds
1 tsp / 5 gm Red chilli powder
1 tsp / 5 gm *Garam masala* powder
1 tsp / 5 gm Turmeric (*haldi*) powder
2 tsp / 10 gm Coriander (*dhaniya*) powder
2 tsp / 10 gm Salt
½ cup / 30 gm Green coriander (*hara dhaniya*) leaves

▸▸ Quality Assurance

- If you have purchased frozen peas, take them out of the freezer well in advance so that they can defrost.
- Wash tomatoes, peeled onion, and green chillies in running water.
- Wait for cooker to depressurize before opening.

▸▸ Execution

Subroutine 1 – Boil potatoes (10 minutes)

- Pressure cook potatoes with skin till 3 whistles. Remove, peel and break into large chunks by squeezing them.

Subroutine 2 – Preparing masala (15 minutes)

- Boil water in a saucepan and add the whole tomatoes. Let the tomatoes remain in the boiling water until the skin begins to split, this usually takes about a minute. Remove the tomatoes immediately, allow cooling and then peel the skin using your fingers. Grind the tomatoes in the blender and set aside (tomato purée).
- Heat the oil in a casserole pot on high flame for 1 minute.
- Add cumin seeds and fry for 20-25 seconds.
- Add red chilli, *garam masala*, turmeric and coriander powders, and salt. Fry for 30 seconds.
- Add tomato purée and peas. Cook for 10 minutes stirring constantly.

Subroutine 3 – Integration (5 minutes)

- Add the potato pieces into the *masala* with 2 cups water and cook for 5 minutes.
- Garnish with chopped green coriander leaves before serving.

▸▸ Testing & Optimization

- If you prefer a thicker consistency for the gravy, you can add 1 cup yoghurt.

▸▸ Suggested Deployment

Aloo matar rasedaar can be eaten with *mooli parathas* (see p. 154) or *puri* (see p. 156) and with a spicy vegetable like *bharwan mirchi* (see p. 111).

BHINDI KADHI

Okra in Gram Flour Curry

Serves 2

High-Level Project Overview

Kadhi originated in Punjab but has gained popularity all over India with each state having its own version. It is a yoghurt-based dish and consequently creamy in texture. There are several variations of this dish but the only key feature that changes is the type of *pakora* or vegetable added. Here I am replacing the commonly used gram flour *pakora* with okra which I prefer.

▶▶ Project Schedule

50 minutes in linear execution mode

▶▶ Inventory & Procurement

250 gm Okra (*bhindi*)
4 tbsp / 40 gm Gram flour (*besan*)
1 cup / 225 gm Yoghurt (*dahi*)
3 tbsp / 45 ml Vegetable oil
1 tsp / 3 gm Mustard seeds (*rai*)
2 Onions, medium-sized
2 stalks Curry leaves (*kadhi patta*)
1 tsp / 5 gm Turmeric (*haldi*) powder
¼ tsp Asafoetida (*hing*) powder
2 tsp / 10 gm Salt
1 tbsp / 15 gm Ghee
1 tsp / 5 gm Red chilli powder

▶▶ Quality Assurance

- When buying okra, bend the ends to test for tenderness. The end should snap when bent. If it bends all the way, the okra has become soft with age.
- Curry leaves must look fresh and green. Old curry leaves will be dry and stiff.
- Wash okra, peeled onions, and curry leaves in running water.

▶▶ Execution

Subroutine 1 – Preparing gravy mix (10 minutes)

- Mix the gram flour with 2 cups water and beat thoroughly, ensuring any balls formed are squished and the mixture attains a smooth, runny texture. Beat in the yoghurt with 2 more cups of water and stir thoroughly. Taste mixture and note the 'raw gram flour' taste, you will need to know this taste in order to determine when to stop cooking the final product. Keep aside.

Subroutine 2 – Preparing vegetables (15 minutes)

- Cut onions into quarters, chop okra into 2" pieces, and strip curry leaves from stalks. Set aside.
- Heat the oil in a casserole pot on high flame for 1 minute.
- Add mustard seeds and allow them to splutter.
- Add okra and onions and fry for 15 minutes, stirring constantly.
- Add curry leaves, turmeric and asafoetida powders. Fry for 30 seconds.

Subroutine 3 – Integration (25 minutes)

- Add yoghurt gram-flour mix from Subroutine 1.
- Add salt and stir well.
- Cook on medium flame for 20-25 minutes; stirring frequently and ensuring the *kadhi* does not stick to the bottom of the pan.
- Heat the ghee in a small pan; add red chilli powder and fry for 5 seconds. Pour over the *kadhi*.

▸▸ Testing & Optimization

- You can replace okra with other options such as radish, vegetable kofta, *pakoras*, etc.
- If you like fenugreek seeds, you can add a few at the seasoning stage along with the mustard seeds.

▸▸ Suggested Deployment

Bhindi kadhi can be eaten with rice or *rotis* and vegetables like *bhindi* fry (see p. 68), *bharwan mirchi* (see p. 111), or *bharwan karela* (see p. 72).

Dry Dishes

BHINDI FRY

Pan-fried Okra

Serves 2

High-Level Project Overview

Simple, unpretentious, delicate and dignified, this vegetable towers over all other vegetables when it comes to a good old cut-and-fry curry (my opinion). During my years in West Africa, I have seen the same reverence being paid to this vegetable by the West African tribes of Nigeria and surrounding countries. In the US, bags of chopped frozen okra are emptied into vegetable stews while in the East it is used in curries in a manner similar to Indians.

▶▶ Project Schedule

30 minutes in linear execution mode

▶▶ Inventory & Procurement

500 gm Okra (*bhindi*)
3 tbsp / 45 ml Vegetable oil
1 Onion, large
2 tsp / 12 gm Ginger-garlic (*adrak-lasan*) paste
1 tsp / 5 gm Red chilli powder
2 tsp / 10 gm Coriander (*dhaniya*) powder
1 tsp / 5 gm *Garam masala* powder
2 tsp / 10 gm Salt

▶▶ Quality Assurance

- When buying okra, bend the ends to test for tenderness. The end should snap when bent. If it bends all the way, the okra has become fibrous with age and consequently unsuitable for this dish.
- Wash okra and peeled onion in running water.
- Dry the washed okra with a clean towel before chopping. If you don't, the sticky mucilage secreted by this vegetable will mix with the residual water and make a mess.

▸▸ Execution

- Cut okra into 1" pieces and slice onions finely.
- Heat the oil in a frying pan on high flame for 1 minute.
- Add onion and ginger-garlic paste; fry till onion turns golden brown.
- Add okra, red chilli, coriander and *garam masala* powders, and salt. Mix ingredients well until okra is well coated with oil and *masala*.
- Reduce flame to medium and fry for 20 minutes till pieces are tender; stir periodically.

▸▸ Testing & Optimization

- I have added onions and ginger-garlic paste for my liking. However, both are optional and can be skipped.
- You can also add juice of one lemon or 1 tsp mango powder to give the dish a tangy taste

▸▸ Suggested Deployment

Bhindi fry can be eaten with rice or *roti* and any flavoured *dal*.

BAINGAN ALOO

Eggplant with Potato

Serves 4

High-Level Project Overview

This dish is a favourite among all Indians alike. Simplicity is the norm and elegance is the taste. Quick to prepare, it's an easy ride from the chopping board to the frying pan and eventually to the meal plate.

▸▸ Project Schedule

30 minutes in linear execution mode

▸▸ Inventory & Procurement

500 gm Eggplant (*baingan*), black beauty variety
2 Potatoes, large
4 tbsp / 60 ml Vegetable oil
1 tsp / 5 gm Turmeric (*haldi*) powder
1 tsp / 5 gm *Garam masala* powder
1 tsp / 5 gm Red chilli powder
2 tsp / 10 gm Coriander (*dhaniya*) powder
2 tsp / 10 gm Salt

▸▸ Quality Assurance

- When buying eggplant ensure the skin is taut and they resound with a hollow note when you strike them with your finger. This means they are tender and fresh. If the skin has wrinkles and sound is a dull thud, they have been sitting on the shelf too long and probably have large inedible seeds inside too.
- Wash eggplant and peeled potatoes in running water before chopping. It's imperative you store the potato and eggplant, during peeling and chopping, in salt water at all times or else they will discolour (due to oxidation) with degradation in taste too.

▸▸ Execution

- Chop eggplant and potatoes into 1" cubes.
- Heat the oil in a frying pan on high flame for 1 minute.
- Add chopped potato pieces and turmeric powder, sauté for 3 minutes.

- Lower flame to medium. Add eggplant pieces, *garam masala,* red chilli and coriander powders, and salt. Mix well so that all the pieces are uniformly coated with oil and *masala*. Place the lid and fry for 20 minutes, stirring frequently.

▸▸ Testing & Optimization

- You can also add some ginger-garlic paste early on. It adds a new dimension of flavour to the dish.

▸▸ Suggested Deployment

Baingan aloo can be eaten with rice, *roti* and any flavoured *dal.*

BHARWAN KARELA

Stuffed Bitter Gourd

Serves 4

High-Level Project Overview

There are many variations of this dish and each has its own uniqueness. In certain North Indian states, bitter gourd is stuffed with mince meat and shallow-fried. It's seldom cooked with any other vegetable due to its bitter taste. Here we make this dish with a simple *masala* stuffing.

▸▸ Project Schedule

45 minutes in linear execution mode

▸▸ Inventory & Procurement

500 gm Bitter gourd (*karela*), small
4 tbsp / 60 ml Vegetable oil

For the stuffing

2 Lemons (*nimbu*)
3 tbsp / 45 gm Andhra peanut powder
2 tsp / 10 gm *Rasam* powder
1 tsp / 5 gm Red chilli powder
2 tsp / 12 gm Ginger-garlic (*adrak-lasan*) paste
1 tbsp / 15 ml Mustard (*sarson*) oil
1 tsp / 2½ gm Carom (*ajwain*) seeds

▸▸ Quality Assurance

- When buying bitter gourd ensure they are green and firm with no yellow patches. Yellowing is an indication of the vegetable ripening, ripe bitter gourd is no good for this dish.
- Wash bitter gourd in running water.

▸▸ Execution

Subroutine 1 – Preparing bitter gourd (10 minutes)

- Make a lengthwise deep incision on each bitter gourd running about 75 per cent of the body length and gouge out the inside flesh using a small knife and your fingers. Keep empty bitter gourd shells and the flesh aside. Do not dispose the seeds; they make a crunchy addition to the final dish.

Subroutine 2 – Preparing stuffing masala (10 minutes)

- Cut and extract juice from the lemons, filter to remove pulp and seeds.

- Mix the ingredients for stuffing into a bowl to make a paste of smooth consistency. If required add oil to get the right consistency. Taste the *masala* and adjust the salt or red chilli powder level.
- Using your fingers, take the *masala* mix and stuff into each bitter gourd.
- Leave some *masala* mix in the bowl and add the flesh and seeds from Subroutine 1.

Subroutine 3 – Frying stuffed bitter gourd (20 minutes)

- Heat 3 tbsp oil in a frying pan on high flame for 1 minute.
- Add the stuffed bitter gourd to the oil, placing them carefully to avoid splattering.
- Roll the bitter gourd using a tong, coating them uniformly with the oil.
- Reduce flame to medium-low and fry for 20 minutes. Periodically rotate the bitter gourd by 90 degrees to ensure all sides get cooked. You will know the bitter gourd is done when a knife passes in and out of the thickest part without much resistance.
- Remove bitter gourd from pan and dispose excess *masala* left inside.

Subroutine 4 – Finishing up (2 minutes)

- Add the remaining oil, bitter gourd flesh, and *masala* to the clean pan. Fry for 2 minutes till the flesh becomes tender.
- Pour the *masala* over the stuffed bitter gourd.

⏩ Testing & Optimization

- You can experiment with the stuffing *masala* by replacing Andhra peanut powder with Andhra curry leaf powder, garlic chutney powder, Andhra gun powder, gram flour with carom seeds, etc.

⏩ Suggested Deployment

Bharwan karela can be eaten with rice and *bhindi kadhi* (see p. 65).

JHATPAT PANEER

Stir-fried Cottage Cheese

Serves 4

High-Level Project Overview

Cottage cheese (*paneer*) and bell peppers (capsicum) have for long been cooked together in India for their perfectly complementing mild tastes, and the cashew nuts have always been a favourite of Mughlai cuisine connoisseurs. Combine these favourites and you have a great blend of tastes that mix interestingly on your taste-buds.

▸▸ Project Schedule

30 minutes in linear execution mode

▸▸ Inventory & Procurement

200 gm Cottage cheese (*paneer*)
1 Red capsicum
1 Yellow capsicum
12 Cashew nuts (*kaju*), large
3 tbsp / 45 ml Vegetable oil
1 tsp / 3 gm Cumin (*jeera*) seeds
1 Onion, large
1 tsp / 6 gm Ginger-garlic (*adrak-lasan*) paste
1 tsp / 5 gm *Garam masala* powder
1 tsp / 5 gm Red chilli powder
1 tsp / 5 gm Turmeric (*haldi*) powder
1 tbsp / 12 gm Dried fenugreek leaves (*kasoori methi*) or 1 bunch fresh leaves
1 tsp / 5 gm Salt

▸▸ Quality Assurance

- Unless you like everything absolutely fresh and homemade, you can buy frozen cottage cheese from the local supermarket. I use frozen cottage cheese packets since they have no preservatives like vinegar in the packing. Ensure to defrost frozen cottage cheese before using.
- When buying capsicum, ensure that they are quite firm to touch and the skin is taut. The stems must be fresh and fleshy. Old capsicum will look shrivelled and de-hydrated.
- Wash capsicum and peeled onion in running water.

▸▸ Execution

- Peel onion and chop roughly into large pieces.
- Cut red and yellow capsicum into approx.imately 1" square pieces.
- Split the cashews into half.
- Cut cottage cheese into 1" cubes (if not already purchased that way).
- Heat the oil in a pan for 1 minute on high flame.
- Add cumin seeds and fry for 20-25 seconds.
- Add the onion and ginger-garlic paste and fry for 1 minute, reduce the flame to medium.
- Add the capsicum, cashew nuts, cottage cheese, *garam masala*, red chilli and turmeric powders, fenugreek and salt. Fry for 15 minutes stirring occasionally.

▸▸ Testing & Optimization

- You can experiment by replacing the cashew nuts with peanuts.
- If you are from North India and like a hint of sweetness in your curries, feel free to throw in some raisins or pieces of chopped pineapple.

▸▸ Suggested Deployment

This dish can be eaten with *parathas* and *rajma masala* (see p. 37).

KURKURI ARVI

Crunchy Colocasia

Serves 4

High-Level Project Overview

This is a tasty dish of colocasia coated with spices and shallow-fried in oil that is infused with the flavour of carom seeds. *Kurkuri arvi* is meant to be eaten as part of a meal, but can be also a finger-food by itself while watching re-runs of X-Files.

▸▸ Project Schedule

30 minutes in linear execution mode

▸▸ Inventory & Procurement

500 gm Colocasia (*arvi*)
6 tbsp / 60 gm Wholewheat (*atta*) flour
1 tsp / 5 gm *Garam masala* powder
1 tsp / 5 gm Red chilli powder
1 tsp / 5 gm Turmeric (*haldi*) powder
2 tsp / 10 gm Coriander (*dhaniya*) powder
1 tsp / 5 gm Mango powder (*amchur*)
1 tsp / 5 gm Salt
5 tbsp / 75 ml Vegetable oil
1 tsp / 2½ gm Carom (*ajwain*) seeds

▸▸ Quality Assurance

- When shopping for colocasia, select tubers with rich and waxy look. Colocasia sitting on the shelves for too long will have a dry look and the packet will have debris inside, this debris is the skin falling off due to dryness.
- Wash colocasia in running water.
- Wait for cooker to depressurize before opening.

▸▸ Execution

- Wash the colocasia thoroughly and cut into approx.imately 2" pieces, leaving the skin on.
- Place pieces in pressure cooker with 1 tsp salt and enough water to cover; pressure cook till 2 whistles.
- Drain the colocasia from the water and peel the skin using your fingers. The skin

should peel off easily. If you can do this while the colocasia is still warm then peeling is easier. Once the colocasia gets cold the skin becomes sticky so peeling is more difficult and time consuming.

- Take one piece of steamed colocasia and place in your left palm. Soft squeeze the colocasia using your right palm until you get a patty of uniform thickness. Do not press too hard, you will break the patty.
- Repeat this process with all the colocasia and set aside.
- Mix the wheat flour, garam *masala*, red chilli, turmeric, coriander and mango powders and salt in a bowl.
- Carefully take one colocasia patty at a time and place in the bowl, covering both sides with the spices. You can gently press the spices into the colocasia patty to help it stick more efficiently.
- Heat the oil in a frying pan for 1 minute on high flame.
- Add the carom seeds and fry for 20-25 seconds.
- Reduce flame to medium. Slowly add a few colocasia patties to the oil. Fry each side till golden brown.
- Remove from the oil and place on tissue or newspaper to help soak the excess oil.
- Continue this frying process until all the colocasia patties are fried.

▸▸ Testing & Optimization

- You can experiment by replacing wheat flour with gram flour or rice flour.

▸▸ Suggested Deployment

Kurkuri arvi can be eaten with rice and *dal* and accompanied with *nariyal ki chutney* (see p. 166).

BANDH GOBI KI SUBZI

Sautéed Cabbage

Serves 4

> **High-Level Project Overview**
>
> If you are looking for a low fat, high vitamin (K & C), and high fibre vegetable to cook for lunch, then look no further. Cabbage is your strategic partner when you feel like cooking less and relaxing more. It cooks fast, tastes as good when raw, and fills your tummy up substantially. There are many varieties of cabbage, and this recipe can be used to make any of these (green, red or white).

▸▸ Project Schedule

30 minutes in linear execution mode

▸▸ Inventory & Procurement

1 Cabbage (*bandh gobi*)

3 tbsp / 45 ml Vegetable oil

1 tsp / 3 gm Mustard seeds (*rai*)

2 tsp / 10 gm Salt

1 tsp / 5 gm Turmeric (*haldi*) powder

2 tsp / 10 gm Coriander (*dhaniya*) powder

1 tsp / 5 gm Red chilli powder

1 tsp / 5 gm *Garam masala* powder

▸▸ Quality Assurance

- Cabbage rots from the outside inwards, so if the exterior leaves look good then the insides are good too. Always peel and dispose the outermost layer of leaves before using the vegetable.
- Wash cabbage in running water.
- Once cut, use up the cabbage as it starts to lose its nutrients quickly.

▸▸ Execution

- Chop cabbage finely.
- Heat the oil in a frying pan on high flame for 1 minute.
- Add mustard seeds and allow them to splutter.
- Add cabbage, salt, turmeric, coriander, red chilli and *garam masala* powders. Mix well till cabbage is well coated with oil and *masala*.

- Sprinkle handful of water into the pan, reduce flame to medium, place lid and allow cooking for 15 minutes. Stir periodically to prevent burning.

▶▶ Testing & Optimization

- You can add some tomato pieces, if desired.

▶▶ Suggested Deployment

Bandh gobi ki subzi can be eaten with rice and *sambar* (see p. 25).

ALOO GOBI

Cauliflower Cooked with Potatoes

Serves 4

High-Level Project Overview

A classic staple dish of Indian cuisine, the cauliflower, for years, has been serving as a mainstay dish known for its simple taste and ease of preparation. It's a vegetable that readily lends itself to be cooked in conjunction with other vegetables such as potatoes, carrots, and other multi-vegetable dishes such as *kormas*.

▸▸ Project Schedule

30 minutes in linear execution mode

▸▸ Inventory & Procurement

1 / 250 gm Cauliflower (*phool gobi*)
2 Potatoes, medium-sized
3 tbsp / 45 ml Vegetable oil
1 tsp / 3 gm Mustard seeds (*rai*)
1 tsp / 3 gm Cumin (*jeera*) seeds
2 tsp / 12 gm Ginger-garlic (*adrak-lasan*) paste
2 stalks Curry leaves (*kadhi patta*)
1 tsp / 5 gm Red chilli powder
1 tsp / 5 gm Turmeric (*haldi*) powder
1 tsp / 5 gm *Garam masala* powder
1 tsp / 5 gm Salt
1 tsp / 5 gm Mango powder (*amchur*)

▸▸ Quality Assurance

- When buying cauliflower, ensure that it is lively white with no discoloured patches on it.
- Wash cauliflower florets and peeled potatoes separately in running water.
- In this dish you will be cooking two vegetables together that do not cook at the same rate. So break the cauliflower into florets which are slightly larger than the potatoes pieces.
- Wait for cooker to depressurize before opening.

▸▸ Execution

- Chop potatoes into 6 pieces each and break cauliflower into large florets.

- Heat the oil in the pressure cooker on high flame for 1 minute.
- Add mustard seeds and allow them to splutter.
- Add cumin seeds and fry for 20-25 seconds.
- Add the potatoes, ginger-garlic paste, and curry leaves; turn down flame to medium and fry for 5 minutes.
- Add the red chilli, turmeric and *garam masala* powders. Fry for 30 seconds.
- Add the cauliflower florets, ½ cup water and salt. Pressure cook till 2 whistles.
- Remove from pressure and add mango powder. Cook for 30 seconds and switch the flame off.

▶▶ Suggested Deployment

Aloo gobi can be eaten with rice or *roti* and accompanied with *rajma masala* (see p. 37), *sambar* (see p. 25) or *dal* and pickle.

BHARWAN BHINDI

Stuffed Okra

Serves 4

High-Level Project Overview

Here is another interesting way of making okra. This dish requires some skill to prepare, especially a stable hand to slice the okra without splitting them.

▸▸ Project Schedule

42 minutes in linear execution mode

▸▸ Inventory & Procurement

500 gm Okra (*bhindi*), short about 4" long

4 tbsp / 60 ml Vegetable oil

For the stuffing:

2 Lemons (*nimbu*)

3 tbsp Andhra peanut powder

¼ tsp Carom (*ajwain*) seeds

2 tsp / 12 gm Ginger-garlic (*adrak-lasan*) paste

1 tsp / 5 gm Red chilli powder

1 tbsp / 15 ml Mustard (*sarson*) oil

▸▸ Quality Assurance

- When buying okra, bend the ends to test for tenderness. The end should snap when bent. If it bends all the way, the okra has become soft with age.
- Wash okra in running water and dry with a towel before slitting. If you don't, the sticky mucilage secreted by this vegetable will mix with the residual water and make a mess.

▸▸ Execution

Subroutine 1 – Preparing okra (10 minutes)

- Make a slit in the middle of each okra running about 75 per cent of its length and set aside.

Subroutine 2 – Preparing stuffing masala (10 minutes)

- Cut and extract juice from the lemons, filter to remove pulp and seeds.
- Mix the ingredients for stuffing in a bowl and make a paste of smooth consistency.

If required, add more oil to get the consistency. Taste the *masala* and adjust salt or red chilli powder level.

- Using your fingers, take the *masala* mix and stuff into each okra. Be careful when prying the okra open as this act could cause the slit to run and split the entire okra.
- Leave some *masala* mix in the bowl.

Subroutine 3 – Frying stuffed okra (20 minutes)

- Heat 3 tbsp oil in a frying pan on high flame for 1 minute.
- Add the stuffed okra to the oil, placing them carefully to avoid splattering the oil.
- Shake the pan to roll the okra, coating them uniformly with the oil.
- Reduce flame to medium and fry for 20 minutes. Stir periodically by shaking the pan (if the okra does not turn over easily use a tong).
- Remove okra from pan and dispose excess *masala* left inside (this *masala* is usually burnt).

Subroutine 4 – Finishing up (2 minutes)

- Add the remaining 1 tbsp oil and the remaining *masala* to the clean pan, fry for 1 minute.
- Pour the *masala* over the okra.

▸▸ Testing & Optimization

- You can experiment with the stuffing *masala* by replacing Andhra peanut powder with *sambar* powder, Andhra curry leaf powder, garlic chutney powder, Andhra gunpowder, etc.

▸▸ Suggested Deployment

Bharwan bhindi can be eaten with rice, *roti* and any mild flavoured curry like *kadhi*, *dal* or *bhein aur aloo masala* (see p. 48).

MASALEDAAR KACCHA KELA

Spicy Green Banana

Serves 4

High-Level Project Overview

Green bananas, also known as plantains, were first consumed in India in 600 BC. Being rich in carbohydrates, vitamin C and A, and several important minerals like potassium, copper, magnesium, calcium, and iron, it is the ideal brain-food for Indian IT engineers. The entire plantain plant is edible, including the flower, fruit and stem.

▸▸ Project Schedule

30 minutes in parallel execution mode

▸▸ Inventory & Procurement

2 / 500 gm Raw bananas (*kaccha kela*)
2 tsp / 10 gm Salt
1 tsp / 5 gm Turmeric (*haldi*) powder
1 Onion, large
2 Green chillies
3 tbsp / 45 ml Vegetable oil
1 tsp / 3 gm Cumin (*jeera*) seeds
2 tsp / 12 gm Ginger-garlic (*adrak-lasan*) paste
1 tsp / 5 gm *Garam masala* powder
2 tsp / 10 gm Coriander (*dhaniya*) powder
1 tsp / 5 gm Mango powder (*amchur*)

▸▸ Quality Assurance

- Apply a little oil to your hands before processing the raw bananas. They secrete a substance that will stick to your skin and clothing, and is very difficult to wash off once it creates a stain.
- Keep chopped banana pieces in salt water.
- Wash tomatoes, peeled onion, and green chillies in running water.
- Wait for cooker to depressurize before opening.
- When adding spice powders to the frying onion paste, wait till the water content in the onion has reduced. You want to fry the spices, not boil them.

▸▸ Execution

Subroutine 1 – Preparing the bananas (10 minutes)

- Peel and cut the bananas into 1" cubes.
- Place banana pieces, 1 tsp salt, and turmeric powder with 2 cups water in a pressure cooker. Cook till 2 whistles.
- Drain excess water and set aside.

Subroutine 2 – Preparing the masala (20 minutes)

- Grind the onion and green chillies into a paste in a blender.
- Heat the oil in a casserole pot on high flame for 1 minute.
- Add cumin seeds and fry for 20-25 seconds.
- Add the onion-green chilli and ginger-garlic pastes to the oil, fry for 10 minutes on medium flame.
- Add *garam masala*, coriander and mango powders and remaining salt. Fry for 30 seconds.

Subroutine 3 – Integration (5 minutes)

- Add the banana pieces to the *masala*.
- Mix thoroughly and cook on medium flame for 5 minutes.

▸▸ Testing & Optimization

- If the dish is not spicy enough, add some red chilli powder to the seasoning.
- You don't have to grind the onions and green chillies. You can also slice them finely and use.

▸▸ Suggested Deployment

Masaledaar kaccha kela can be eaten with rice and *sambar* (see p. 25) or *rasam* (see p. 27).

BHEIN MAZEDAAR

Stir-fried Lotus Stem with Spring Onion Serves 4

High-Level Project Overview

This is a simple dish of sliced lotus stem fried with fresh spring onions and spices.

▸▸ Project Schedule

30 minutes in linear execution mode

▸▸ Inventory & Procurement

2 Lotus stems (*bhein*), medium-sized
2 bunches Spring onions (*hara pyaz*)
3 tbsp / 45 ml Vegetable oil
1 tsp / 3 gm Cumin (*jeera*) seeds
1 tsp / 5 gm *Garam masala* powder
1 tsp / 5 gm Red chilli powder
1 tsp / 5 gm Turmeric (*haldi*) powder
1 tsp / 5 gm Salt
1 tsp / 5 gm Mango powder (*amchur*)

▸▸ Quality Assurance

- Wash lotus stems and spring onions in running water.

▸▸ Execution

- Cut and discard the top ¼" and roots of the spring onions.
- Slice the green section of the onion into 2" pieces.
- Slice the white section of the onion into quarters.
- Slice the lotus stem into ¼" pieces.
- Heat the oil in a frying pan for 1 minute on high flame.
- Add cumin seeds and fry for 20-25 seconds.
- Add the lotus stem, *garam masala*, red chilli and turmeric powders, and salt. Fry for 3 minutes.
- Sprinkle a handful of water and cover the dish. Simmer for 15 minutes on low flame, stirring occasionally, adding more water if necessary.

- Remove the lid, add the spring onions and fry for 5 minutes on high flame.
- Add mango powder before switching the flame off.

▸▸ Suggested Deployment

Bhein mazedaar can be eaten with rice or *rotis* accompanied with *lobiya masala* (see p. 40).

ALOO BEANS

Flat Beans Sautéed with Potatoes

Serves 4

High-Level Project Overview

The flat or velore bean known in the West as Lima beans, is large and flat with plenty of flesh. Popular in South Indian *thalis*, these beans make a great combination with potatoes.

▶▶ Project Schedule

30 minutes in linear execution mode

▶▶ Inventory & Procurement

500 gm Flat beans
2 Potatoes, medium-sized
3 tbsp / 45 ml Vegetable oil
1 tsp / 3 gm Mustard seeds (*rai*)
1 tsp / 3 gm Cumin (*jeera*) seeds
1 tsp / 6 gm Ginger-garlic (*adrak-lasan*) paste
1 tsp / 5 gm Red chilli powder
1 tsp / 5 gm Turmeric (*haldi*) powder
1 tsp / 5 gm *Garam masala* powder
2 tsp / 10 gm Salt
1 tsp / 5 gm Mango powder (*amchur*)

▶▶ Quality Assurance

- When buying flat beans, ensure that they are young and flat. If they look very bulgy where the seeds are inside, then the bean has matured making the rest of the pod very fibrous. They should also snap when bent.
- Wash beans and potatoes in running water.
- Keep chopped potato in salt water to prevent oxidation.

▶▶ Execution

- Peel and cut potatoes into 1" cubes.
- Using a small knife, cut one end of the bean pod 99 per cent of the way through and drag the snipped piece away from the pod, it's the best way of removing the fibrous binding thread that holds the bean pod together. Repeat the same for the other end of the bean and all the beans.

- Cut the beans into 1" pieces and set aside.
- Heat the oil in a frying pan on high flame for 1 minute.
- Add mustard seeds and allow them to splutter.
- Add cumin seeds and fry for 20-25 seconds.
- Add potato pieces and ginger-garlic paste. Reduce flame to medium and fry for 5 minutes.
- Add beans, red chilli, turmeric and garam *masala* powders, and salt. Lid the pan and cook for 15 minutes on medium flame stirring frequently.
- Remove lid and add mango powder. Cook for 1 minute more before switching the flame off.

▸▸ Suggested Deployment

Aloo beans can be eaten with rice or *roti* and accompanied with *tadka dal* (see p. 23).

TINDORA FRY

Stir-fried Ivy Gourd

Serves 2

High-Level Project Overview

The English name for *tindora* is Gentleman's Toes or Ivy Gourd. In Andhra Pradesh, where it is hugely popular, it's known as *dondakaya* and is fried with spices. *Tindora* resembles a tiny cucumber and has a mild unique taste. It is generally not cooked with other vegetables.

▸▸ Project Schedule

30 minutes in linear execution mode

▸▸ Inventory & Procurement

500 gm Ivy Gourd (*tindora*)
3 tbsp / 45 ml Vegetable oil
2 tsp / 12 gm Ginger-garlic (*adrak-lasan*) paste
1 tsp / 5 gm Red chilli powder
2 tsp / 10 gm Coriander (*dhaniya*) powder
1 tsp / 5 gm *Garam masala* powder
2 tsp / 10 gm Salt

▸▸ Quality Assurance

- When buying ivy gourd, ensure that they are green and raw (break one and look inside). Ripe ones turn bright yellow / orange in colour.
- Wash ivy gourd in running water.

▸▸ Execution

- Cut ivy gourd into thin slices.
- Heat the oil in a frying pan on high flame for 2 minutes.
- Add ivy gourd and ginger-garlic paste. Fry for 5 minutes.
- Add red chilli, coriander and *garam masala* powders, and salt. Mix all the ingredients well till ivy gourd is well coated with oil and *masala*.
- Fry for 20 minutes till pieces are tender; stir periodically.

⏩ Testing & Optimization

- You can also toss in chopped onion if you like.

⏩ Suggested Deployment

Tindora fry can be eaten with rice or *roti* and any *tadka dal* (see p. 23).

BESANI HARA PYAZ

Spring Onion Cooked with Gram flour Serves 4

High-Level Project Overview

Gram flour is ground chickpeas with a heavy nutty flavour that changes drastically the taste of any dish it is added to. Mostly used as batter for deep-fried snacks and thickener for soups and gravies, its very high protein content makes it an ideal choice for the muscle-building Indian IT engineer.

▸▸ Project Schedule

20 minutes in linear execution mode

▸▸ Inventory & Procurement

10 Spring onions (*hara pyaz*)
5 tbsp / 75 gm Vegetable oil
1½ tbsp / 25 gm Butter
1 tsp / 3 gm Mustard seeds (*rai*)
3" piece Ginger (*adrak*)
1 tsp / 5 gm Red chilli powder
2 tsp / 10 gm Coriander (*dhaniya*) powder
½ tsp / 2½ gm *Garam masala* powder
1 tsp / 5 gm Salt
5 tbsp / 50 gm Gram flour (*besan*)
1 tsp / 5 gm Mango powder (*amchur*)

▸▸ Quality Assurance

- Snip away roots and wash spring onions in running water.
- When chopping spring onions, include the green leaves up to 75 per cent of their length.
- Scrape ginger with a knife to remove skin before chopping into pieces.
- Wash ginger and spring onions in running water.
- Gram flour, when added to oil, will absorb a lot of the oil. You have to add more oil as you see necessary to keep the ingredients frying.

▸▸ Execution

- Chop spring onions into 1" pieces and grate ginger. Set aside.

- Heat the oil and butter in a pan on medium heat till butter melts. The addition of oil to the butter will prevent the butter from burning.
- Add mustard seeds and allow them to splutter.
- Add grated ginger, red chilli, coriander and *garam masala* powders and salt. Fry for 1 minute.
- Add the gram flour and fry till it turns deep golden.
- Add the chopped spring onion and mix thoroughly (add more oil if necessary). Cook for another 15 minutes stirring frequently.
- Add mango powder 1 minute before switching flame off.

▸▸ Testing & Optimization

- You can experiment with the spices like replacing red chilli powder with black pepper powder or peppercorns.

▸▸ Suggested Deployment

Besani hara pyaz can be eaten with rice and *roti* and accompanied with *tadka dal* (see p. 23).

ANDA BHURJI

Spicy Scrambled Eggs

Serves 4

High-Level Project Overview

A popular worldwide dish that saved countless bachelors from the drudgery of cumbersome cooking, scrambled egg can be made in less than 15 minutes. A versatile dish that can be eaten with rice, bread, *rotis* or straight up.

▸▸ Project Schedule

15 minutes in linear execution mode

▸▸ Inventory & Procurement

8 Eggs

2 tbsp / 30 ml Vegetable oil

1 Onion, medium-sized

1 Green chilli

1 Tomato, medium-sized

¼ tsp Turmeric (*haldi*) powder

Red chilli powder to taste

1 tsp / 5 gm Salt

¼ cup / 15 gm Green coriander (*hara dhaniya*) leaves

▸▸ Quality Assurance

- Wash peeled onion, green chilli, tomato, and coriander leaves in running water.
- Eggs cook very fast, use medium to low flame and stir constantly.

▸▸ Execution

- Finely chop onion, green chilli, and tomatoes. Set aside.
- Heat the oil in a frying pan on high flame for 1 minute.
- Add onion and green chilli, fry till golden brown.
- Reduce flame to medium. Add tomato pieces, turmeric and red chilli powders, and salt.
- Mix thoroughly and cook for 5-7 minutes.
- Break eggs into the pan and stir constantly till eggs and *masala* mix thoroughly. Cook for 2 minutes and remove from flame.
- Garnish with chopped green coriander leaves, before serving.

▸▸ Testing & Optimization

- You can replace chopped green chillies with black pepper powder.

▸▸ Suggested Deployment

Anda bhurji can be eaten with *parathas* and pickle.

TURAI KI SUBZI

Spicy Stir-fried Ridge Gourd

Serves 4

High-Level Project Overview

Ridge gourd is known as *turai* in Hindi and *beerakai* in Telugu. With a tough rugged skin on the outside and soft cucumber-like flesh inside, ridge gourd has a distinct flavour of its own. Also known as Loofah Gourd, when ripe and dry its body turns into a mesh of tough golden fibres which are used as a scrub. In Andhra Pradesh, its skin is also used to make delicious chutneys to be consumed with *idlis*.

▸▸ Project Schedule

30 minutes in linear execution mode

▸▸ Inventory & Procurement

1 Ridge gourd (*turai*), large
3 tbsp / 45 ml Vegetable oil
1 Onion, large
1 tsp / 5 gm Turmeric (*haldi*) powder
1 tsp / 5 gm Red chilli powder
2 tsp / 10 gm Coriander (*dhaniya*) powder
1 tsp / 5 gm Cumin (*jeera*) powder
1 tsp / 5 gm Salt

▸▸ Quality Assurance

- Ridge gourds turn fibrous when ripe, so make sure you buy tender ones.

▸▸ Execution

- Peel and chop the gourd into 1" pieces.
- Chop onion finely.
- Heat the oil in a frying pan on high flame for 1 minute.
- Add onion and turmeric powder. Fry till golden brown.
- Add ridge gourd, red chilli, coriander and cumin powders, and salt. Mix well so that the gourd pieces are uniformly coated with *masala* and oil.
- Place lid on the pan and reduce flame to medium, cook for 15 minutes stirring periodically.

- Remove lid and cook for another 5 minutes to let the excess moisture evaporate.

▸▸ Testing & Optimization

- You can add some tomato pieces, if desired.

▸▸ Suggested Deployment

Turai subzi can be eaten with rice and *tadka dal* (see p. 23), or plain *roti* and pickle.

BHARWAN BAINGAN

Stuffed Baby Eggplant

Serves 4

High-Level Project Overview

Stuffed eggplant has a venerable position in Indian cuisine and is prepared extensively during gala festivals and celebrations. The original recipe is quite complex to follow as it includes roasting several types of lentils and pulses, powdering them, mixing and matching, etc. Here we will be using some ready-made powders instead.

▸▸ Project Schedule

47 minutes in linear execution mode

▸▸ Inventory & Procurement

500 gm Purple eggplants (*baingan*), small, round

4 tbsp / 60 ml Vegetable oil

For the stuffing

2 tbsp Andhra peanut powder

2 tsp / 10 gm *Rasam* powder

2 tsp / 12 gm Ginger-garlic (*adrak-lasan*) paste

1 tsp / 2½ gm Carom (*ajwain*) seeds

2 Lemons (*nimbu*)

1 tbsp / 15 ml Mustard (*sarson*) oil

▸▸ Quality Assurance

- When buying eggplants ensure the skin is taut and they resound with a hollow note when you strike them with your finger. This means they are tender and fresh. If the skin has wrinkles and the sound is a dull thud, they have been sitting on the shelf for too long and probably have large inedible seeds formed inside. Also, the stem must look lively green and not wear a wilted dark colour.
- Wash in running water. It is imperative you keep the eggplants, after cutting, in salt water or else they discolour (oxidation) with slight degradation in taste.

▸▸ Execution

Subroutine 1 – Preparing eggplants (5 minutes)

- Hold the eggplant in your hand upside down and make a vertical cut starting at its base running 75 per cent through to its stem. Turn the eggplant in your hand and make another similar cut so that you get a '+' shape slit.

- Repeat for all eggplants and store in salted water.

Subroutine 2 – Preparing stuffing masala (10 minutes)

- Cut and extract juice from the lemons, filter to remove pulp and seeds.
- Mix the ingredients for stuffing in a bowl and make a paste of smooth consistency. If required add more oil to get the consistency. Taste the *masala* and adjust salt.
- Using your fingers, take the *masala* mix and stuff into each eggplant.
- Leave some *masala* mix in the bowl.

Subroutine 3 – Frying stuffed eggplants (30 minutes)

- Heat 3 tbsp oil in a pan on high flame for 1 minute.
- Add stuffed eggplants to the oil, placing them carefully to avoid splattering oil.
- Roll the eggplants by holding the stalks, coating them uniformly with the oil.
- Reduce flame to low and fry for 30 minutes. Periodically rotate the eggplants by 90 degrees to ensure all sides get cooked.
- Remove eggplants from pan and dispose excess *masala* left inside.

Subroutine 4 – Finishing up (2 minutes)

- Add the remaining 1 tbsp oil and *masala* to the clean pan. Fry for 1 minute.
- Pour the *masala* over the eggplants.

▸▸ Testing & Optimization

- Andhra peanut powder, *rasam* and carom seeds have their own unique strong flavour. If you wish a milder taste, use only Andhra peanut powder, *rasam* powder or *sambar* powder. Retain the carom seeds no matter which powder you decide to go with.

▸▸ Suggested Deployment

Bharwan baingan can be eaten with rice or *roti* and accompanied with *tadka dal* (see p. 23) or *bhindi kadhi* (see p. 65).

BHUNI BORBOTI

Stir-fried String Beans and Potatoes

Serves 4

High-Level Project Overview

First used domestically in Mesoamerica (Mexico and Central America) and introduced to the East in the fifteenth century, the string bean is grown for the thick flesh of its pod rather than the beans inside which are quite small in size. Low in calories and high on vitamins and minerals, it is an ideal food for the weight-conscious Indian IT engineers.

▸▸ Project Schedule

30 minutes in linear execution mode

▸▸ Inventory & Procurement

250 gm String beans
2 Potatoes, medium-sized
3 tbsp / 45 ml Vegetable oil
1 tsp / 3 gm Mustard (*rai*) seeds
1 tsp / 3 gm Cumin (*jeera*) seeds
1 tsp / 6 gm Ginger-garlic (*adrak-lasan*) paste
1 tsp / 5 gm Red chilli powder
1 tsp / 5 gm Turmeric (*haldi*) powder
1 tsp / 5 gm *Garam masala* powder
2 tsp / 10 gm Salt
1 tsp / 5 gm Tamarind (*imli*) paste

▸▸ Quality Assurance

- Wash beans and potatoes in running water.
- Keep chopped potato pieces in salt water to prevent oxidation.

▸▸ Execution

- Peel and cut potatoes into 1" cubes.
- Cut beans into 1" pieces. Set aside.
- Heat the oil in a pan on high flame for 1 minute.
- Add mustard seeds and allow them to splutter.
- Add cumin seeds and fry for 10 seconds.

- Add potato pieces and ginger-garlic paste. Reduce flame to medium and fry for 5 minutes.
- Add red chilli, turmeric and *garam masala* powders, and salt. Fry for 30 seconds.
- Add beans and tamarind paste; mix thoroughly. Lid the pan and cook for 15 minutes on low flame stirring frequently.

▸▸ Testing & Optimization

- If you do not like tamarind, you can replace it with mango powder.

▸▸ Suggested Deployment

This dish can be eaten with rice and *rotis* and accompanied with *dal*, *bhindi kadhi* (see p. 65), *chana masala* (see p. 34) or *rajma masala* (see p. 37).

PYAZ PATTI

Tangy Onion Sprouts

Serves 2

High-Level Project Overview

Leafy sprouts from germinating onion bulbs are edible and valued more if they are topped by the immature white flower. While the taste is similar to spring onions, the onion sprouts do not have the developing onion bulb at the base. Onion sprouts form an important part of salads, sauces, and relishes in cuisines around the world.

▸▸ Project Schedule

30 minutes in linear execution mode

▸▸ Inventory & Procurement

2 bundles Onion sprouts
3 Tomatoes, large
3 tbsp / 45 ml Vegetable oil
2 tbsp / 17 gm Peanuts (*moongphalli*)
2 tsp / 12 gm Ginger-garlic (*adrak-lasan*) paste
2 stalks Curry leaves (*kadhi patta*)
1 tsp / 5 gm Red chilli powder
1 tsp / 5 gm Turmeric (*haldi*) powder
2 tsp / 10 gm Coriander (*dhaniya*) powder
1 tsp / 5 gm Salt
1 tsp / 5 gm Tamarind (*imli*) paste

▸▸ Quality Assurance

- Wash tomatoes and onion sprouts in running water.

▸▸ Execution

- Chop onion sprouts and tomatoes into 1" pieces.
- Heat the oil in a pan on medium flame for 1 minute.
- Add peanuts and fry for 3 minutes.
- Add onion sprouts and ginger-garlic paste. Reduce flame to medium and fry for 5 minutes.
- Add curry leaves, red chilli, turmeric and coriander powders, and salt. Fry for 30 seconds.

- Add tomatoes, tamarind paste, and 1 cup water. Mix thoroughly, lid the pan and cook for 10 minutes stirring occasionally.

▶▶ Suggested Deployment

Pyaz patti can be eaten with rice or *roti* and *raita* of your choice.

MILIJULI SUBZI

Vegetable Medley

Serves 4

High-Level Project Overview

A popular preparation to make when there are little quantities of various vegetables left in the refrigerator. It is a highly nutritious dish that takes very little time and effort to make.

►► Project Schedule

30 minutes in linear execution mode

►► Inventory & Procurement

200 gm Green beans
200 gm Carrots (*gajar*)
200 gm Cauliflower (*phool gobi*)
200 gm Capsicum (*Shimla mirch*)
3 tbsp / 45 ml Vegetable oil
1 tsp / 5 gm Turmeric (*haldi*) powder
2 tsp / 10 gm Salt
1 tsp / 5 gm Red chilli powder
2 tsp / 10 gm *Tandoori masala* powder
1 tbsp / 10 gm Coconut (*nariyal*), dessicated
½ cup / 100 ml Coconut milk

►► Quality Assurance

- Wash all vegetables in running water.

►► Execution

- Chop vegetables into 1" pieces. Set aside.
- Heat the oil in a casserole pot on high flame for 1 minute.
- Add all the vegetables, turmeric powder, and salt. Cover with lid and cook for 15 minutes, stirring frequently.
- Add red chilli and *tandoori masala* powders, cook for 1 minute.
- Add desiccated coconut and coconut milk. Reduce flame to medium and cook for 10 minutes, stirring frequently.

►► Testing & Optimization

- You can replace the dessicated coconut and coconut milk with tomato purée and mashed garlic cloves, it is another entirely new way of making vegetable medley.

►► Suggested Deployment

Milijuli subzi can be eaten with rice or *parathas* and pickle.

DAHI BHINDI

Fried Okra in Yoghurt

Serves 4

High-Level Project Overview

Okra reminds me of my childhood days in Nigeria, where the okra is consumed copiously in a popular soup called Gumbo. This Indian dish, however, comprises of tender okra pieces fried to near crisp perfection immersed in rich yoghurt gravy and flavoured with aromatic carom seeds. Yum!

▸▸ Project Schedule

30 minutes in linear execution mode

▸▸ Inventory & Procurement

250 gm Okra (*bhindi*)
2 cups / 450 gm Yoghurt (*dahi*)
3 tbsp / 45 ml Vegetable oil
powder
2 tbsp / 17 gm Peanuts (*moongphalli*)
1 tsp / 2½ gm Carom (*ajwain*) seeds

1 Onion, large
3" piece Ginger (*adrak*)
½ tsp / 2½ gm Black pepper (*kali mirch*)
2 tsp / 10 gm Coriander (*dhaniya*) powder
1 tsp / 5 gm Salt

▸▸ Quality Assurance

- Scrape ginger with a knife to remove skin before chopping into pieces.
- Wash ginger, okra and peeled onion in running water.
- I like to use sour yoghurt as it lends a tangy flavour to the dish.

▸▸ Execution

- Cut okra into 1" pieces, chop onions and ginger finely, and dilute yoghurt with 1 cup water. Set aside.
- Heat the oil in a frying pan on medium flame for 1 minute.
- Add peanuts, fry for 3 minutes.
- Add carom seeds and fry for 20-25 seconds.

- Add onion and ginger pieces, fry till onions turn golden brown.
- Add okra, black pepper and coriander powders, and salt. Reduce flame to medium and fry for 15 minutes, stirring frequently.
- Switch off flame and allow cooling for 5 minutes.
- Add yoghurt, mix thoroughly.

▸▸ Testing & Optimization

- You can replace black pepper with red chilli powder or chopped green chillies.
- You can replace chopped ginger with ginger-garlic paste.

▸▸ Suggested Deployment

Dahi bhindi can be eaten with rice, *roti* and pickle.

DUM ALOO

Baby Potatoes in Yoghurt

Serves 4

High-Level Project Overview

A North Indian dish prepared widely on special occasions (due to time and effort required). This dish is essentially boiled baby potatoes flavoured in a gravy of onions, tomatoes and spices. Effort is well rewarded with outstanding taste.

▸▸ Project Schedule

42 minutes in parallel execution mode

▸▸ Inventory & Procurement

1 kg Baby potatoes
4 Tomatoes, medium-sized
4 tbsp / 60 ml Vegetable oil
1 tsp / 3 gm Cumin (*jeera*) seeds
4 Cloves (*laung*)
4 Green cardamom (*choti elaichi*)
1 stick Cinnamon (*dalchini*)
2 Bay leaves (*tej patta*), large
½ tsp / 2½ gm Asafoetida (*hing*) powder
2 Onions, medium-sized
2 tsp / 12 gm Ginger-garlic (*adrak-lasan*) paste
1 tsp / 5 gm *Garam masala* powder
1 tsp / 5 gm Turmeric (*haldi*) powder
1 tsp / 5 gm Red chilli powder
2 tsp / 10 gm Coriander (*dhaniya*) powder
2 tsp / 10 gm Salt
1 cup / 225 gm Yoghurt (*dahi*)
½ cup / 30 gm Green coriander (*hara dhaniya*) leaves
2 tbsp / 30 ml Cream, fresh

▸▸ Quality Assurance

- When you shop for potatoes for this dish, ask for *dum aloo* variety. Shop keepers know what that means and will give you a packet of small round ones specially meant for this dish.
- Wash potatoes, tomatoes, peeled onions, and coriander leaves in running water.
- Wait for cooker to depressurize before opening.
- When adding spice powders to the frying onion paste, wait till the water content in the onions has reduced. You want to fry the spices, not boil them.

▸▸ Execution

Subroutine 1 – Preparing potatoes (20 minutes)

- Place potatoes with skin in pressure cooker and cook till 1 whistle.
- Remove from pressure cooker, peel the skin and gently pierce each potato with a fork (the holes made by the fork will allow the *masala* to penetrate the potato). Set aside.

Subroutine 2 – Preparing masala (30 minutes)

- Boil water in a saucepan and add the whole tomatoes. Let the tomatoes remain in the boiling water until the skin begins to split, this usually takes about a minute. Remove the tomatoes immediately, allow cooling and then peel the skin using your fingers. Blend the tomatoes in a blender. Set aside.
- Grind the onions into a paste in a blender (do not add water as the onions have enough natural water content inside them). Set aside.
- Heat the oil in a casserole pot on high flame for 1 minute.
- Add cumin seeds, cloves, green cardamom, cinnamon stick, bay leaves, and asafoetida. Fry for 1 minute.
- Add the onion and ginger-garlic pastes to the oil, fry for 10 minutes on medium flame till all the water content has evaporated (you will know this when the paste starts to turn brown and sticks to the bottom of the pan).
- Add the *garam masala*, turmeric, red chilli and coriander powders, and salt. Fry for 30 seconds.
- Add tomato purée and cook for further 10 minutes, stirring constantly. The longer you leave this *masala* the more concentrated it becomes and emanates more flavours. If you have the time to let it cook longer then turn the flame to a simmer. At this point the *masala* looks deep brown in colour and starts to stick to the pan as all the moisture has evaporated.

Subroutine 3 – Integration (10 minutes)

- Add the potatoes to the *masala*.
- Add 2-3 cups water, lid the pot and cook for 10 minutes. Switch the flame off.
- Take some of the gravy in a separate bowl and add the yoghurt, mix thoroughly and return the mix to the main dish. This is to prevent the yoghurt from curdling due to drastic temperature change.
- Garnish with chopped fresh coriander leaves and cream before serving.

▸▸ Testing & Optimization

- This is a complex dish that allows much variation. You can experiment by adding other spices such as black cardamom, caraway seeds, black peppercorns, poppy seeds, mace, nutmeg, etc.

▸▸ Suggested Deployment

Dum aloo can be eaten with rice and *rotis* and accompanied with *bhindi fry* (see p. 68)

BHARWAN MIRCHI

Stuffed Anaheim Peppers

Serves 4

High-Level Project Overview

This tangy, spicy and unconventional dish will spice up any meal. The Anaheim pepper is a perfect vegetable for stuffing, with a medium heat range and enough body to hold the stuffing.

▸▸ Project Schedule

30 minutes in linear execution mode

▸▸ Inventory & Procurement

6 Anaheim peppers
2 Lemons (*nimbu*)
4 tbsp Andhra peanut powder
1 tbsp / 18 gm Ginger-garlic (*adrak-lasan*) paste
½ tsp / 2½ gm Red chilli powder
3 tbsp / 45 ml Vegetable oil

▸▸ Quality Assurance

- Wash peppers in running water.

▸▸ Execution

- Cut and extract juice from the lemons, filter to remove pulp and seeds. Set aside.
- Make an incision lengthwise running 75 per cent the length on each pepper.
- Using your fingers and a small knife, pry open each pepper and remove the seeds to the extent possible without tearing the pepper. Set aside.
- Mix the Andhra peanut powder, ginger-garlic paste, red chilli powder, and lemon juice in a bowl.
- Stuff this mix in each pepper.
- Heat the oil in a frying pan on medium flame for 1 minute.
- Sauté the peppers till they brown uniformly on all sides.

▸▸ Testing & Optimization

- You can try experimenting extensively with the stuffing. I often replace the peanut powder with various other *masala* powders like garlic rice mix, curry leaf *masala* powder, Andhra gunpowder, etc. Sometimes I combine two powders with complementing flavours.
- You can replace the lemon juice with tamarind to get a more earthy taste.

▸▸ Suggested Deployment

Bharwan mirchi can be eaten with rice and *roti* and with any mildly flavoured dishes like *dal*, *kadhi* or *matar paneer* (see p. 61). Do not serve with any dish that has a strong flavour and will conflict with the taste of the stuffing and chilli, like *sambar*.

BHARWAN BAINGAN KISHTI

Spinach in Eggplant Boats — Serves 4

High-Level Project Overview

Stuffed eggplant is a popular dish in many continents and through history. In the West it is often combined with cheese and baked, and in India it is stuffed with spices and shallow-fried. I cooked up this dish while racking my brain for innovative ways to make spinach. In addition to great taste, my method of preparation has high presentation value making the dish an excellent addition to a dinner party.

▸▸ Project Schedule

35 minutes in linear execution mode

▸▸ Inventory & Procurement

1 Eggplant (*baingan*), black beauty variety
2 bundles Spinach (*palak*)
2 Onions, large
4 tbsp / 60 ml Vegetable oil
1 tsp / 3 gm Cumin (*jeera*) seeds
1 tsp / 2 gm Coriander (*dhaniya*) seeds
10 Garlic (*lasan*) cloves
½ tsp Turmeric (*haldi*) powder
1 tsp / 5 gm Red chilli powder
1 tsp / 5 gm *Garam masala* powder
1 tsp / 5 gm Tamarind (*imli*) paste
2 tbsp / 30 ml Cream, fresh

▸▸ Quality Assurance

- Wash eggplant, onions, and spinach in running water.
- When adding spice powders to the frying onion paste, wait till the water content in the onions has reduced. You want to fry the spices, not boil them.

▸▸ Execution

Subroutine 1 – Preparing eggplant shells (5 minutes)

- Remove the crown and cut the eggplant into half lengthwise. Using a spoon gouge out 75 per cent of the flesh from each half. You will now have two hollow eggplant shells. Dunk the two shells in salt water and set aside.

- Chop the eggplant flesh into small pieces, set aside.

Subroutine 2 – Preparing stuffing (25 minutes)

- Grind onions into a paste in a blender (do not add water as the onions have enough natural water content inside them). Set aside.
- Chop spinach finely, set aside.
- Slightly mash garlic by hitting them once with a flat utensil, slit green chillies lengthwise. Set aside.
- Heat 2 tbsp oil in a frying pan on high flame for 1 minute.
- Add cumin and coriander seeds; fry for 20-25 seconds.
- Reduce flame to medium. Add onion paste and garlic; fry till onions turn golden brown.
- Add the chopped spinach, eggplant flesh, turmeric, red chilli, and *garam masala* powders. Lid the pan and cook for 15 minutes.
- Add tamarind paste and cook for a further 1 minute.

Subroutine 3 – Frying stuffed eggplant shells (20 minutes)

- Take the eggplant shells and fill the hollow with the *masala* from Subroutine 2.
- Place the shells back in the same pan, add the rest of the oil, sprinkle some water over them and cover with a lid. Reduce flame to low and cook for 15 minutes. Move the shells around occasionally and sprinkle more water, if required.
- Switch off flame and garnish with fresh cream. Cut shells into quarters before serving.

▸▸ Suggested Deployment

Bharwan baingan kishti can be eaten with *parathas* and *aloo pyaz raita* (see p. 163).

KELE KE PHOOL KI SUBZI

Stir-fried Banana Florets Serves 2

High-Level Project Overview

Plantains were first consumed in India in 600 BC. Being rich in carbohydrates, vitamin C, vitamin A, and several important minerals like potassium, copper, magnesium, calcium, and iron, it is the ideal brain-food for the Indian IT engineers. This dish requires a labour-of-love effort, processing the flower to extract the edible parts is time-consuming, complex and the yield is low.

▸▸ Project Schedule

55 minutes in linear execution mode

▸▸ Inventory & Procurement

2 Banana flowers
1 tsp / 5 gm Salt
½ tsp / 2½ gm Turmeric (*haldi*) powder
3 tbsp / 45 ml Vegetable oil
1 tsp / 3 gm Mustard seeds (*rai*)
1 Onion, large
1 Green chilli
1 tsp / 6 gm Ginger-garlic (*adrak-lasan*) paste
1 tsp / 5 gm Andhra peanut powder

▸▸ Quality Assurance

- Apply a little oil to your hands before processing the banana flower. The flower secretes a substance that will stick to your skin and clothing, and is very difficult to wash off once it creates a stain.
- Wash banana florets, peeled onion, and green chilli in running water.
- Wait for cooker to depressurize before opening.

▸▸ Execution

Subroutine 1 – Preparing flower (30 minutes)

- Peel the large purple bracts of the flowers away and extract the florets inside.
- With your fingers, pry open each floret and remove the stamen from inside. You

can recognize the stamen by its bulky head and its toughness (will not snap when tugged).

- Place banana florets, 1 tsp salt, and turmeric powder with 2 cups water in pressure cooker and steam for 2 whistles.
- Drain excess water and set aside.

Subroutine 2 – Preparing masala (20 minutes)

- Chop onion and green chilli finely.
- Heat the oil in a casserole pot on high flame for 1 minute.
- Add mustard seeds and allow them to splutter.
- Reduce flame to medium. Add the onion, green chilli, and ginger-garlic paste to the oil, fry till onion turns golden brown.

Subroutine 3 – Integration (5 minutes)

- Add the banana florets to the *masala* and fry for 5 minutes.
- Add the peanut powder, fry for 1 minute and switch the flame off.

⏩ Testing & Optimization

- Andhra peanut powder has salt in it, so I am not adding any additional salt to this dish except when pressure cooking the florets. Adjust salt, if necessary.
- If spice is insufficient, add some red chilli powder to the seasoning.

⏩ Suggested Deployment

Kele ke phool ki subzi can be eaten with rice and *tadka dal* (see p. 23).

KARELA FRY

Fried Bitter Gourd

Serves 2

High-Level Project Overview

Bitter gourd, known as *karela* in Hindi and *kakarakai* in Telugu, is the most bitter vegetable and definitely an acquired taste. The bitterness can be removed partially by soaking in buttermilk, but then what's the point? This vegetable is sometimes cooked with a heavy load of spices to mask its bitter taste, however, I like the bitterness so here I describe a simple method.

▸▸ Project Schedule

30 minutes in linear execution mode

▸▸ Inventory & Procurement

500 gm Bitter gourd (*karela*)
1 Onion, large
3 tbsp / 45 ml Vegetable oil
2 tsp / 12 gm Ginger-garlic (*adrak-lasan*) paste
2 tsp / 10 gm Coriander (*dhaniya*) powder
1 tsp / 5 gm Red chilli powder
1 tsp / 5 gm *Garam masala* powder
2 tsp / 10 gm Salt

▸▸ Quality Assurance

- When buying bitter gourd ensure that they are green and firm with no yellow patches. Yellowing is an indication of the vegetable ripening, ripe bitter gourd is no good.
- Wash bitter gourd and peeled onion in running water.

▸▸ Execution

- Cut bitter gourd into thin slices (chips style) and chop onion finely.
- Heat the oil in a frying pan on high flame for 1 minute.
- Add onion and ginger-garlic paste. Fry till onion turns golden brown.
- Add bitter gourd, coriander, red chilli and *garam masala* powders, and salt. Mix ingredients well until the bitter gourd is well coated with oil and *masala*.

- Reduce flame to medium and fry for 15 minutes, stirring periodically, till pieces are tender.

▸▸ Testing & Optimization

- I have added onions and ginger-garlic paste for my liking. However, both are optional and you can skip them.
- You can add some carom seeds, as its flavour goes well with the bitterness of bitter gourd.

▸▸ Suggested Deployment

Karela fry can be eaten with rice, *tadka dal* (see p. 23) and lemon pickle.

BHARWAN SHIMLA MIRCH

Stuffed Capsicum

Serves 4

High-Level Project Overview

Capsicum, also known as bell peppers, are ideal for stuffing. In Spanish and Creole cuisine, bell peppers are stuffed with flavoured rice or meat mince topped with cheese. There are many variations to what the stuffing is made of, I like a tangy potato mash. If you are weight conscious, you can bake the capsicum instead of frying them.

▸▸ Project Schedule

50 minutes in parallel execution mode

▸▸ Inventory & Procurement

3 Green capsicum (*Shimla mirch*)
2 Potatoes, medium-sized
6 tbsp / 90 ml Vegetable oil
2 tsp / 6 gm Mustard seeds (*rai*)
1 tsp / 3 gm Cumin (*jeera*) seeds
¼ tsp Asafoetida (*hing*) powder
½ tsp / 2½ gm Turmeric (*haldi*) powder
1 tsp / 5 gm Red chilli powder
1 tsp / 5 gm *Garam masala* powder
2 tsp / 10 gm Salt
2 tsp / 10 gm Tamarind (*imli*) paste

▸▸ Quality Assurance

- When buying capsicum, ensure they are quite firm to touch and the skin is taut. The stems must be fresh and fleshy. Old capsicum will look shrivelled and de-hydrated.
- Wash capsicum and peeled potatoes in running water.
- Wait for cooker to depressurize before opening.

▸▸ Execution

Subroutine 1 – Preparing capsicum (5 minutes)

- Using a small knife, pierce the capsicum next to its stem and cut around the stem creating a circular incision. You should be able to pull the stem out completely now along with most of the seeds. A hole is left on the top of the vegetable. The rest of the capsicum is intact in its original shape.

- Repeat the procedure for the other capsicums. Set aside.

Subroutine 2 – Preparing potato (10 minutes)

- Place potatoes with skins in a pressure cooker with enough water to cover, add 1 tsp salt. Pressure cook till 3 whistles.
- Remove, peel and using a masher, mash till soft and smooth.

Subroutine 3 – Preparing tamarind masala (10 minutes)

- Dilute tamarind paste with 1 cup water. Set aside.
- Heat 2 tbsp oil in a frying pan on high flame for 1 minute.
- Add mustard seeds and allow them to splutter.
- Add cumin seeds and fry for 20-25 seconds.
- Add asafoetida, turmeric, red chilli and *garam masala* powders, and salt. Fry for 1 minute.
- Add the tamarind water and boil on high flame till it thickens to a paste; stir constantly.
- Add mashed potato and mix thoroughly.

Subroutine 4 – Frying stuffed capsicum (30 minutes)

- Stuff seasoned potato mash into the capsicums through the hole in the top.
- Heat 4 tbsp oil in a casserole pot and place the capsicum in. Sprinkle a handful of water on them and lid the pan.
- Reduce the flame to low and cook for 20-25 minutes, turning them 90 degrees to ensure all sides get evenly cooked (capsicum flesh must yield easily if you poke it with a knife).

▸▸ Testing & Optimization

- You can experiment with the seasoning by replacing red chilli powder with chopped green chillies.
- You can add some finely chopped onions to the mashed potatoes, if desired.
- You can add some gram flour to the mashed potatoes, if desired.

▸▸ Suggested Deployment

Bharwan Shimla mirch can be eaten with rice and *chana dal* (see p. 29) or with *parathas* and *dal makhni* (see p. 31).

DAHI LAUKI

Snake Gourd in Yoghurt

Serves 4

High-Level Project Overview

Snake gourd, known as *lauki* in Hindi and *potlakai* in Telugu, is predominantly found in Southeast Asian climates. It's an easy vegetable to cook since its mild flavour complements a range of other vegetables.

▸▸ Project Schedule

30 minutes in linear execution mode

▸▸ Inventory & Procurement

1 / 500 gm Snake gourd (*lauki*)
3 tbsp / 45 ml Vegetable oil
1 tsp / 3 gm Mustard seeds (*rai*)
1 Onion, large
2 tsp / 12 gm Ginger-garlic (*adrak-lasan*) paste
1 tsp / 5 gm Red chilli powder
2 tsp / 10 gm Coriander (*dhaniya*) powder
1 tsp / 5 gm Salt
2 cups / 450 gm Yoghurt (*dahi*)

▸▸ Quality Assurance

- When buying snake gourd, ensure it has retained its tubular shape and is firm to touch. When you bend the snake gourd it must snap. Old snake gourd will collapse, bend without breaking and also develop soft spots.
- Wash the snake gourd in running water before chopping.
- The flesh of the snake gourd is some what mucilaginous, so beware of your clothes when chopping this vegetable.

▸▸ Execution

- Chop the snake gourd into 1" pieces and the onion finely.
- Heat the oil in a frying pan on high flame for 1 minute.
- Add mustard seeds and allow them to splutter.
- Add onion and ginger-garlic paste and fry till onion turns golden brown.

- Reduce flame to medium. Add snake gourd pieces, red chilli and coriander powders, and salt. Mix well, cover pan with lid and cook for 15 minutes; stir occasionally.
- Turn the flame off and allow cooling for 10 minutes (check the snake gourd pieces, they must be soft).
- Add yoghurt and mix well.

▶▶ Testing & Optimization

- You can replace red chilli powder with black pepper powder or 2 slit green chillies.
- You can add some peanuts at the seasoning stage, they go well with yoghurt.

▶▶ Suggested Deployment

Dahi lauki can be eaten with rice and *bharwan bhindi* (see p. 82) or *bharwan karela* (see p. 72).

BHUNA GAJAR

Stir-fried Carrot

Serves 4

High-Level Project Overview

The first recorded observations of carrot as an edible vegetable dates back to the tenth century BC. It is a rich source of vitamin A, dietary fibre, antioxidants, and minerals (highly recommended for the perennially eye-strained IT engineers). This preparation has a sweet taste, so tweak it with spices.

▸▸ Project Schedule

30 minutes in linear execution mode

▸▸ Inventory & Procurement

500 gm Carrots (*gajar*)
3 tbsp / 45 ml Vegetable oil
1 tsp / 3 gm Mustard seeds (*rai*)
¼ tsp Asafoetida (*hing*) powder
½ tsp / 2½ gm Turmeric (*haldi*) powder
1 tsp / 5 gm *Garam masala* powder
1½ tsp / 7½ gm Red chilli powder
1 tsp / 5 gm Salt

▸▸ Quality Assurance

- When shopping for carrots, look for bright orange ones which are tight and stiff. Old carrots discolour, shrivel and lose their firmness (won't snap when bent).

▸▸ Execution

- Heat the oil in a frying pan on high flame for 1 minute.
- Add mustard seeds and allow them to splutter.
- Add the carrots, asafoetida, turmeric, *garam masala* and red chilli powders, and salt. Mix well till all carrot pieces are well coated with oil and *masala*.
- Sprinkle a handful of water into the pan, reduce flame to medium, place lid and allow cooking for 15 minutes. Stir frequently.

▸▸ Suggested Deployment

Bhuna gajar can be eaten with rice and *sambar* (see p. 25) or *rasam* (see p. 27).

BAINGAN BHARTA

Roasted Spiced Eggplant　　Serves 4

High-Level Project Overview

Roasted eggplant seasoned with spices has been a revered dish through the ages in many countries. The Arabs called this dish *babaghanouj* and the Greeks call it *melitzanosalata*. In India, it is prepared as *baingan bharta*.

▶▶ Project Schedule

40 minutes in parallel execution mode

▶▶ Inventory & Procurement

1 / 500 gm (approx.) Eggplant (*baingan*)

4 Tomatoes, medium-sized

2 Onions, medium-sized

2 Green chillies

3 tbsp / 45 ml Vegetable oil

2 tsp / 12 gm Ginger-garlic (*adrak-lasan*) paste

1 tsp / 5 gm *Garam masala* powder

1 tsp / 5 gm Red chilli powder

1 tsp / 5 gm Turmeric (*haldi*) powder

2 tsp / 10 gm Coriander (*dhaniya*) powder

2 tsp / 10 gm Salt

½ cup / 30 gm Green coriander (*hara dhaniya*) leaves

▶▶ Quality Assurance

- Wash eggplant, tomatoes, peeled onions, green chillies, and coriander leaves in running water.
- When roasting eggplant, use medium flame so that heat penetrates deep into the eggplant.
- Beware of escaping steam from the eggplant, it can cause severe burns.
- When adding spice powders to the frying onion paste, wait till the water content in the onions has reduced. You want to fry the spices, not boil them.

▶▶ Execution

Subroutine 1 – Roasting eggplant (20 minutes)

- Place the full eggplant sideways directly on the gas flame and roast on medium flame. Turn eggplant 90 degrees every 2 minutes until all sides are done (skin turns black, flaky and the eggplant collapses).

- Transfer into a container and delicately peel off the skin. Mash the flesh into a pulp using a masher or fork and set aside.

Subroutine 2 – Preparing masala (30 minutes)

- Boil water in a saucepan and add tomatoes. Let them remain in the boiling water until the skin begins to split (1 minute). Remove immediately, cool and peel the skin using your fingers. Blend into a smooth paste in a blender and set aside.
- Grind the onions and green chillies into a paste in a blender (do not add water as the onions have enough natural water content inside them).
- Heat the oil in a casserole pot on high flame for 1 minute.
- Add the onion-green chilli and ginger-garlic pastes to the oil, fry for 10 minutes on medium flame till all the water content has evaporated (you will know this when the paste starts to turn brown and sticks to the bottom of the pan).
- Add *garam masala*, red chilli, turmeric and coriander powders, and salt. Fry for 30 seconds.
- Add tomato purée and cook for further 10 minutes, stirring constantly. The longer you leave this *masala* the more concentrated it becomes and emanates more flavours. If you have the time to let it cook longer then turn the flame to a simmer. At this point the *masala* looks deep brown in colour and starts to stick to the pan as all the moisture has evaporated.

Subroutine 3 – Integration (5 minutes)

- Add the eggplant pulp from Subroutine 1 to the *masala*.
- Mix thoroughly and cook for 5 minutes.
- Garnish with chopped fresh coriander leaves before serving.

▸▸ Suggested Deployment

Baingan bharta can be eaten with rice or *roti* and pickle.

KELE KA TANA

Banana Stem Subzi

Serves 4

> **High-Level Project Overview**
>
> The banana plant flowers only once in its life after which the pseudo stem is cut down for various uses. The main trunk of the plant is opened up and layers are peeled off to reveal the core stem which is cooked in several ways across India.

▸▸ Project Schedule

45 minutes in parallel execution mode

▸▸ Inventory & Procurement

6"-8"-long Banana stem
2 tsp / 10 gm Salt
1 tsp / 5 gm Turmeric (*haldi*) powder
3 tbsp / 45 ml Vegetable oil
1 Onion, medium-sized
3" piece Ginger (*adrak*)
2 stalks Curry leaves (*kadhi patta*)
2 Green chillies
1 tsp / 5 gm Cumin (*jeera*) powder
2 tsp / 10 gm Coriander (*dhaniya*) powder
1 cup / 450 gm Yoghurt (*dahi*)

▸▸ Quality Assurance

- Apply a little oil to your hands before processing the banana stem. The stem secretes a substance that will stick to your skin and clothing, and is very difficult to wash off once it creates a stain.
- Scrape ginger with a knife to remove skin before chopping into pieces.
- Wash banana stem, peeled onion, green chillies, and ginger in running water.
- Wait for cooker to depressurize before opening.

▸▸ Execution

Subroutine 1 – Preparing banana stem (30 minutes)

- Remove the outer layers of the stem till only the core is left.
- Cut the core stem into ¼"-thick slices (discs) and further cut each slice into stripes.

- Place in pressure cooker with 1 tsp salt, turmeric powder and 2 cups water. Pressure cook till 2 whistles.
- Drain excess water and set aside.

Subroutine 2 –Preparing masala (20 minutes)

- Chop onion, green chillies, and ginger into small pieces.
- Heat the oil in a casserole pot on high flame for 1 minute.
- Add onion and ginger, fry till onion turns golden brown.
- Add curry leaves, green chillies, cumin and coriander powders, and salt. Fry for 30 seconds.

Subroutine 3 – Integration (5 minutes)

- Add the banana stem pieces to the *masala* and cook for 5 minutes or till the pieces absorb the spice flavours.
- Switch off the flame and allow cooling for 10 minutes.
- Dilute yoghurt with 1 cup water and add. Mix well.

▶▶ Testing & Optimization

- If spice is insufficient, add some red chilli powder to the seasoning.

▶▶ Suggested Deployment

Kele ka tana can be eaten with rice and pickle.

PUNJABI TINDA

Spicy Apple Gourd

Serves 4

High-Level Project Overview

Apple gourd (*tinda*), a squash-family vegetable, native to India and Pakistan is used frequently in making dry and wet curries. As with any squash, its mild submissive flavour enables it to be cooked in infinite ways. Please do not confuse *tinda* with *tindora* or *tindla*, which are also known as Gentleman's Toes or Ivy Gourd. *Tinda* is a green round apple-sized gourd.

▸▸ Project Schedule

30 minutes in linear execution mode

▸▸ Inventory & Procurement

6 / 500 gm (approx.) Apple gourd (*tinda*)
3 tbsp / 45 ml Vegetable oil
1 tsp / 3 gm Cumin (*jeera*) seeds
1 Onion, large
1 tsp / 6 gm Ginger-garlic (*adrak-lasan*) paste
1 tsp / 5 gm *Garam masala* powder
1 tsp / 5 gm Red chilli powder
1 tsp / 5 gm Turmeric (*haldi*) powder
2 tsp / 10 gm Coriander (*dhaniya*) powder
1 tsp / 5 gm Salt
4 tbsp / 60 ml Water

▸▸ Quality Assurance

- Wash the apple gourd and peeled onion in running water.

▸▸ Execution

- Roughly chop onion into large pieces and set aside.
- Cut the apple gourd into ¼" pieces and set aside.
- Heat the oil in a frying pan for 1 minute on high flame.
- Add cumin seeds and fry for 20-25 seconds.
- Reduce the flame to medium. Add the onion and ginger-garlic paste, fry for 2 minutes.
- Add the apple gourd, *garam masala*, red chilli, turmeric, and coriander powders,

and salt. Mix thoroughly till the apple gourd pieces are evenly coated with oil and *masala*.

- Sprinkle a handful of water and cover the dish. Cook for 15 minutes on low flame, stirring occasionally.

▸▸ Testing & Optimization

- You can experiment by adding some tomato pieces or purée to the dish.
- You can add a few drops of lemon juice to give the dish a tangy taste.

▸▸ Suggested Deployment

This preparation can be eaten with rice or *roti* and accompanied with any *dal*.

Rice Dishes

SADA CHAWAL

Steamed Rice

Serves 2

High-Level Project Overview

White rice is undoubtedly a bastion of Indian cuisine. This dish forms the platform on which the complete meal is built. So let's start with learning how to make basic white rice. Your grandmother must have made it in quite a different way, but I am not your grandmother so here is my way.

⏩ Project Schedule

10 minutes in linear execution mode

⏩ Inventory & Procurement

2 cups / 400 gm Basmati rice

4 cups / 1 lt Water

⏩ Quality Assurance

- Wash the required portion of rice in running tap water at least once. Drain out water completely or else residual water from washing will upset rice-water ratio at the time of cooking.
- If you have purchased unpackaged rice, sift through for small stones and other foreign particles.
- Where mentioned, please ensure to lower or raise flame as instructed.
- The trick with preparing fluffy rice is the 1:2 ratio of rice to water combined. I prefer Basmati rice to any other type, it simply tastes better and the individual rice grains do not stick to one another when cooked. This method of cooking rice is called the 'Absorption Method'.

⏩ Execution

- Place rice and water in a saucepan and bring to the boil on full flame.
- Place lid on pan as soon as the water starts to boil, then reduce the flame to the lowest possible setting and cook until the rice has absorbed all the water. This generally takes 10 minutes.

- Take a fork and separate the rice till you can see the bottom of the pan; there must be no water or moisture left. Eat a few grains of the cooked rice; you must not perceive an uncooked feel in the middle of the grain. If you perceive rawness, sprinkle a handful of water on the rice and continue cooking for a minute or 2.

▸▸ Testing & Optimization

- There are various methods employed to cook rice. In some parts of India, rice is boiled in plenty of water and the excess water, which is starch water, is drained and used for other preparations.

▸▸ Suggested Deployment

Rice is a foundation dish and can be served with any combination of curry, vegetables, *raita*, pickle, etc.

NIMBU KA PULIHORA

Lemon Rice

Serves 2

High-Level Project Overview

I take great pleasure in preparing and serving this dish at parties I host. It's a bachelor (or hurried couple) friendly dish due to its simplistic nature, great spicy-sour taste and ease of preparation. A warning: I love both ginger and lemon, so I've used both in copious quantities in this dish. If you do not relish these ingredients, you may want to reduce their respective quantities.

▸▸ Project Schedule

20 minutes in parallel execution mode

▸▸ Inventory & Procurement

2 cups / 400 gm Basmati rice
6 Lemons (*nimbu*)
4 tbsp / 60 ml Vegetable oil
2 tsp / 6 gm Mustard seeds (*rai*)
2 tbsp / 25 gm Bengal gram (*chana dal*)
4 tbsp / 30 gm Peanuts (*moongphalli*)
5" piece Ginger (*adrak*)
4 Green chillies
1 tsp / 5 gm Turmeric (*haldi*) powder
¼ tsp Asafoetida (*hing*) powder
2 stalks Curry leaves (*kadhi patta*)
2 tsp / 10 gm Salt

▸▸ Quality Assurance

- Curry leaves must look fresh and green. Old curry leaves will be dry and stiff, avoid these.
- Scrape ginger with a knife to remove skin before chopping into pieces.
- Wash the rice, ginger, green chillies, and curry leaves in running water.
- Where mentioned, please ensure to lower or raise the flame as instructed.
- To get good lemon rice, it's essential that the rice is cooked till no water is left, so the grains separate and no sogginess remain.

▸▸ Execution

Subroutine 1 – Preparing rice (10 minutes)

- Cook the rice as described on page 132.

Subroutine 2 – Preparing seasoning (16 minutes)

- Finely chop ginger, slit green chillies, and strip curry leaves from stalk. Set aside.
- Cut and extract juice from the lemons, filter to remove pulp and seeds. Set aside.
- Heat the oil in a casserole pot on high flame for 1 minute.
- Add mustard seeds and allow them to splutter.
- Add Bengal gram and peanuts, lower flame to medium and fry for 3 minutes or till peanuts turn golden brown.
- Add the ginger and cook the mixture for another 2 minutes, stirring frequently.
- Add the green chillies and let the mixture cook for another 1 minute, stirring frequently.
- Add the turmeric powder, asafoetida, and curry leaves. Stir well for 30 seconds and switch off the flame.

Subroutine 3 – Integration (2 minutes)

- Add cooked rice, lemon juice and salt to the seasoning. Stir well until rice is uniformly coated.

▸▸ Testing & Optimization

- You can experiment with seasoning by adding 1 tsp black gram (*urad dal*).
- You can replace green chillies with dry red chillies.

▸▸ Suggested Deployment

Nimbu ka pulihora can be eaten by itself or with yoghurt.

TAMATAR KA PULAO

Tomato Rice

Serves 2

High-Level Project Overview

Tomato rice is an excellent dish to prepare on days when you open the fridge and knock your head in frustration for forgetting (or being plain lazy) to shop. But if you have followed my best practices in resource management, chances are you will find tomatoes and onions in the vegetable drawer!

▶▶ Project Schedule

30 minutes in parallel execution mode

▶▶ Inventory & Procurement

2 cups / 400 gm Basmati rice
6 Tomatoes, medium-sized
3 tbsp / 45 ml Vegetable oil
2 tsp / 6 gm Mustard seeds (*rai*)
1 tsp / 3 gm Cumin (*jeera*) seeds
2 tbsp / 15 gm Peanuts (*moongphalli*)
1 Onion, large
1 tsp / 6 gm Ginger-garlic (*adrak-lasan*) paste
1 tsp / 5 gm Turmeric (*haldi*) powder
½ tsp / 2½ gm Red chilli powder
2 tsp / 10 gm Coriander (*dhaniya*) powder
¼ tsp Asafoetida (*hing*) powder
2 stalks Curry leaves (*kadhi patta*)
2 tsp / 10 gm Salt

▶▶ Quality Assurance

- Tomatoes must be firm, uniformly red and have a fresh look. Spoilt tomatoes are soft and smelly.
- Curry leaves must look fresh and green. Old curry leaves will be dry and stiff, avoid these.
- Wash the rice, tomatoes, and curry leaves in running water.
- Where mentioned, please ensure to lower or raise the flame as instructed.

▶▶ Execution

Subroutine 1 – Preparing rice (10 minutes)

- Cook the rice as described on page 132.

Subroutine 2 – Preparing tomato gravy (25 minutes)

- Chop tomatoes and onion into small pieces and strip curry leaves from stalk. Set aside.
- Heat the oil in a casserole pot on high flame for 1 minute.
- Add mustard seeds and allow them to splutter.
- Add cumin seeds and fry for 20-25 seconds.
- Add peanuts and lower the flame to medium; fry for 3 minutes or till peanuts turn golden brown.
- Add onion and ginger-garlic paste, fry for 2 minutes.
- Add turmeric, red chilli, coriander, and asafoetida powders, and curry leaves. Stir well for 30 seconds.
- Add tomatoes and salt, mix well and cover the pan. Stir occasionally and cook till tomatoes turn into paste (about 15 minutes).

Subroutine 3 – Integration (2 minutes)

- Add cooked rice to the tomato gravy. Stir well until rice is uniformly coated.

▸▸ Testing & Optimization

- You can experiment with seasoning by adding 1 tsp black gram (*urad dal*).
- You can get a tangy taste by adding 2-3 tsp lemon juice to the gravy.

▸▸ Suggested Deployment

Tamatar ka pulao can be eaten by itself or with *sada dal* (see p. 22).

IMLI KA PULIHORA

Tamarind Rice

Serves 2

High-Level Project Overview

This is one of South India's favourite travel dishes – it's easy to make in large quantities, stays fresh for a long time and the whole family loves it. You are likely to find picnicking families at waterfalls and temples sitting down in a circle to unpack copious quantities of tamarind rice into plates made with dried leaves (or banana leaves). The acidic content of tamarind prevents bacteria from attacking the dish, hence its longevity.

▸▸ Project Schedule

30 minutes in parallel execution mode

▸▸ Inventory & Procurement

2 cups / 400 gm Basmati rice
2 tsp / 10 gm Tamarind (*imli*) paste
3 tbsp / 45 ml Vegetable oil
2 tsp / 6 gm Mustard seeds (*rai*)
3 tbsp / 25 gm Peanuts (*moongphalli*)
1 tbsp / 12 gm Bengal gram (*chana dal*)
4" piece Ginger (*adrak*)
4 Green chillies, large
1 tsp / 5 gm Turmeric (*haldi*) powder
¼ tsp Asafoetida (*hing*) powder
2 stalks Curry leaves (*kadhi patta*)
2 tsp / 10 gm Salt

▸▸ Quality Assurance

- Don't bother soaking and squeezing tamarind like ma and grandma, tamarind paste is available in most leading supermarkets.
- Scrape ginger with a knife to remove skin before chopping into pieces.
- Wash the rice, ginger, green chillies, and curry leaves in running water.
- Curry leaves must look fresh and green. Avoid using old curry leaves that are dry.
- Where mentioned, please ensure to lower or raise the flame as instructed.

▶▶ Execution

Subroutine 1 – Preparing rice (10 minutes)

- Cook the rice as described on page 132.

Subroutine 2 – Preparing tamarind masala (25 minutes)

- Dilute tamarind paste with 2 cups water, finely chop ginger, slit green chillies lengthwise, and strip curry leaves from stalks. Set aside.
- Heat the oil in a casserole pot on high flame for 1 minute.
- Add mustard seeds and allow them to splutter.
- Add peanuts and Bengal gram, lower the flame to medium and fry for 3 minutes or till peanuts turn golden brown.
- Add ginger and green chillies; fry for 1 minute.
- Add turmeric powder, asafoetida, and curry leaves. Fry for 30 seconds.
- Add diluted tamarind paste and salt. Let the gravy boil and thicken into a paste (about 15 minutes).

Subroutine 3 – Integration (2 minutes)

- Add cooked rice to the tamarind gravy. Stir well until rice is uniformly coated.

▶▶ Testing & Optimization

- You can experiment with seasoning by adding 1 tsp black gram (*urad dal*).
- You can increase spice-level by adding couple of dry red chillies in addition to green chillies while preparing seasoning.

▶▶ Suggested Deployment

Imli ka pulihora can be eaten by itself or with yoghurt.

MATAR PULAO

Rice Cooked with Peas

Serves 2

High-Level Project Overview

Also known as *pilaf*, this dish with its origins in Central Asia quickly became popular in the Middle East where scarcity of water forced people to cook several ingredients together. The Indian *pulao* is essentially one or two vegetables seasoned with spices, into which raw rice is added, fried for a few minutes and then cooked with water. The rice absorbs these flavours during the cooking process. The *pulao* is a popular dish across India, with each region customizing it to its own cultural influences.

▸▸ Project Schedule

30 minutes in linear execution mode

▸▸ Inventory & Procurement

2 cups / 400 gm Basmati rice
250 gm Green peas (*hara matar*)
1 tbsp / 15 ml Vegetable oil
2 tbsp / 30 gm Ghee / Butter
2 tsp / 6 gm Mustard seeds (*rai*)
6 Cloves (*laung*)
4 Cardamom (*elaichi*)
2 Onions, medium-sized
2 Green chillies
½ tsp / 2½ gm Black pepper (*kali mirch*) powder
2 tsp / 10 gm Salt

▸▸ Quality Assurance

- If using fresh peas, remove peas from the pods and wash thoroughly. If using frozen peas, defrost them in a microwave oven or just remove from freezer about an hour before preparing the dish.
- Wash peeled onion in running water.
- Wash the rice and drain all water. This is important as any water left at the bottom of the dish will affect the overall water-rice ratio later.

⏩ Execution

- Finely chop onions, slit green chillies lengthwise, and crush the cardamom. Set aside.
- Place oil and butter in a casserole pot and heat on high flame for 1 minute. The addition of oil to the butter will prevent the butter from burning.
- Add mustard seeds, cloves, and cardamom. Fry till the seeds splutter.
- Add onions and green chillies; fry for 10 minutes on medium flame until onions turn golden brown.
- Now add the rice, peas, and black pepper powder; fry for 10 minutes stirring constantly on medium flame.
- Add 4 cups water and salt and bring to the boil on high flame. As soon as the water begins to boil, reduce flame to lowest setting, cover pan with a lid and allow to cook for 15 minutes or till all the water is absorbed.

⏩ Testing & Optimization

- You can replace the black pepper powder with red chilli powder and add some turmeric powder; it will give a very different taste.
- You can add more vegetables like carrots and beans, if desired.
- You can replace some of the water with normal milk or coconut milk.

⏩ Suggested Deployment

Matar pulao can be eaten with pickle, *raita* and roasted poppadoms.

VANGI BAHT

Eggplant Rice

Serves 2

High-Level Project Overview

This popular South Indian dish of flavoured rice and eggplant is excellent for times when you want to cook one tasty dish in a large quantity. Its an ideal choice for family picnics as the high spice content acts as a preservative enabling the dish to stay fresh for a long period of time.

▸▸ Project Schedule

30 minutes in parallel execution mode

▸▸ Inventory & Procurement

2 long Green eggplants (*baingan*)
or 1 large Purple eggplant
2 cups / 400 gm Basmati rice
3 tbsp / 45 ml Vegetable oil
2 tsp / 6 gm Mustard seeds (*rai*)
2 tbsp / 25 gm Bengal gram (*chana dal*)
3 Green chillies
1 tsp / 5 gm Turmeric (*haldi*) powder
¼ tsp Asafoetida (*hing*) powder
2 tsp / 10 gm *Vangi baht masala* powder
2 stalks Curry leaves (*kadhi patta*)
2 tsp / 10 gm Tamarind (*imli*) paste
2 tsp / 10 gm Salt

▸▸ Quality Assurance

- Don't bother soaking and squeezing tamarind like ma and grandma, tamarind paste is available in most leading supermarkets.
- Wash the rice, eggplants, green chillies, and curry leaves in running water.
- Curry leaves must look fresh and green. Avoid dry and old curry leaves.

▸▸ Execution

Subroutine 1 – Preparing rice (10 minutes)

- Cook the rice as described on page 132.

Subroutine 2 – Preparing eggplant masala (25 minutes)

- Chop eggplant into cubes, slit green chillies lengthwise, dilute tamarind paste with ½ cup water, and strip curry leaves from stalk. Set aside.

- Heat the oil in a casserole pot on high flame for 1 minute.
- Add mustard seeds and allow them to splutter.
- Add Bengal gram, lower flame to medium; fry for 2 minutes or till they turn golden brown.
- Add green chillies, turmeric powder, asafoetida, *vangi bath masala* powder, and curry leaves. Fry for 1 minute.
- Add eggplant pieces, tamarind water, and salt; mix well. Cook till eggplant pieces are soft but not pasty (about 15 minutes).

Subroutine 3 – Integration (2 minutes)

- Add cooked rice to the eggplant *masala*. Stir well until rice is uniformly coated.

▶▶ Testing & Optimization

- You can increase spice-level by adding couple of dry red chillies in addition to green chillies while preparing the seasoning.
- You can experiment with seasoning by adding 1 tsp black gram (*urad dal*).

▶▶ Suggested Deployment

This dish can be eaten by itself or with yoghurt or *sada dal* (see p. 22)

THAYIR SADAM

Yoghurt Rice

Serves 2

High-Level Project Overview

Accidentally discovered by nomadic Arabian tribesmen, yoghurt is widely used as a body coolant in the hot tropical weather of India and to balance off the pungent spices commonly used in Indian cuisine. Seasoned yoghurt rice, also known as *thayir sadam* down South, is frequently consumed for breakfast, lunch and dinner.

▸▸ Project Schedule

20 minutes in parallel execution mode

▸▸ Inventory & Procurement

2 cups / 400 gm Basmati rice
400 gm Yoghurt (*dahi*)
2 tbsp / 30 ml Vegetable oil
1 tsp / 3 gm Mustard seeds (*rai*)
1 tbsp / 8 gm Peanuts (*moongphalli*)
2" piece Ginger (*adrak*)
2 Green chillies
2 Dry red chillies (*sookhi lal mirch*)
2 stalks Curry leaves (*kadhi patta*)
2 tsp / 10 gm Salt

▸▸ Quality Assurance

- Scrape ginger with a knife to remove skin before chopping into pieces.
- Wash the rice, ginger, green chillies, and curry leaves in running water.
- Curry leaves must look fresh and green. Old curry leaves will be dry and stiff, avoid these.

▸▸ Execution

Subroutine 1 – Preparing rice (10 minutes)

- Cook the rice as described on page 132.

Subroutine 2 – Preparing seasoning (15 minutes)

- Finely chop ginger, slit green chillies lengthwise, and remove curry leaves from stalks. Set aside.

- Heat the oil in a casserole pot on high flame for 1 minute.
- Add mustard seeds and allow them to splutter.
- Add peanuts, reduce flame to medium and fry till they turn golden brown.
- Add ginger, green chillies, dry red chillies, and curry leaves; fry for another 1 minute.
- Remove from heat and keep aside to cool for 2 minutes.

Subroutine 3 – Integration (2 minutes)

- Add cooked rice, yoghurt, and salt to the seasoning. Stir well.

▸▸ Testing & Optimization

- You can get innovative and experiment by adding various ingredients like Bengal gram, cashew nuts, etc.

▸▸ Suggested Deployment

Thayir sadam can be eaten with pickle or vegetables like *bhindi fry* (see p. 68) and *baingan aloo* (see p. 70).

Indian Breads

SADA ROTI

Pan Roasted Bread

Serves 2

High-Level Project Overview

This is a foundation dish; unsalted, unleavened bread made of wholewheat flour. Quick and easy to make (though it is messy with the flour all over the kitchen table and yourself), *rotis* can be made in huge numbers and stored away for consumption later. Eaten with just about any vegetable, curry or *dal* you will find in this book, this versatile bread along with rice is the backbone of Indian cuisine.

▸▸ Project Schedule

30 minutes in linear execution mode

▸▸ Inventory & Procurement

4 cups / 600 gm Wholewheat (*atta*) flour

Jug of water

▸▸ Quality Assurance

- If this is the first time you are making *rotis*, the disc may not exactly turn out a circle. Don't worry about that, practice makes perfect.
- Store *rotis* in a thermoware container lined with cloth or paper. The thermoware container keeps the *rotis* warm while the cloth or paper absorbs the steam preventing them from getting soggy.

▸▸ Execution

- Place the flour in a bowl and slowly add some water.
- Knead the mixture and continue to add little water, at a time, until a non-sticky dough forms.
- Transfer the dough into an airtight container and refrigerate for at least 15 minutes. As the dough is required to set, it is advised that you make it 15 minutes before commencing.
- Heat a griddle (*tawa*) on medium flame.

- Put some flour on a plate and set it near your work area. Call this Plate A.
- While the griddle is heating, make approx. 8-10 1.5" diameter balls from dough.
- Take one ball and dust it with the flour on Plate A, rotate it so all sides are coated with dry flour. The purpose of this action is to make the dough ball non-sticky.
- Using a rolling pin (*belan*) roll out into an approx. 7" disc. If the dough sticks to the rolling pin while being rolled out, flip the dough in flour from Plate A again.
- Place the *roti* on the griddle and turn it over when bubbles start appearing (in about 1 minute).
- After roasting the *roti* for about 30 seconds on the second side, turn it again.
- Now press the *roti* gently down using a clean paper or cloth towel. The *roti* should puff up as you press it.
- Remove from pan and repeat the same process with remaining dough balls (you can start rolling out the second dough ball even as the first is still roasting on the pan. This, however, requires multi-tasking ability or else you will burn the *rotis*).

▸▸ Testing & Optimization

- *Roti* can also be directly roasted over an open flame, it is called *phulka*.

▸▸ Suggested Deployment

Roti can be eaten with any vegetable, *dal*, or curry dish.

SADA PARATHA

Pan-fried Bread

Serves 2

High-Level Project Overview

The *paratha* is a bigger cousin of the *roti*. It is much thicker and is pan-fried with ghee.

▸▸ Project Schedule

30 minutes in linear execution mode

▸▸ Inventory & Procurement

4 cups / 600 gm Wholewheat (*atta*) flour

½ tsp / 2½ gm Salt

4 tbsp / 60 gm Ghee

Jug of water

▸▸ Quality Assurance

- If this is the first time you are making *parathas*, the disc may not exactly turn out a circle. Don't worry about that, practice makes perfect.
- Store *parathas* in a thermoware container lined with cloth or paper. The thermoware container keeps the *parathas* warm while the cloth or paper absorbs the steam preventing them from getting soggy.

▸▸ Execution

- Place the flour in a bowl and slowly add some water.
- Knead the mixture and continue to add little water, at a time, until a non-sticky dough forms.
- Transfer the dough into an airtight container and refrigerate for at least 15 minutes. As the dough is required to set, it is advised that you always make it 15 minutes before commencing cooking your meal.
- Heat a griddle (*tawa*) on medium flame.
- Put some flour on a plate and set it near your work area. Call this Plate A.
- While the griddle is heating make approx. 6-8 2" diameter balls from the dough.
- Take one ball and dust it with the flour on Plate A, rotate it so all sides are coated

with dry flour. The purpose of this action is to make the dough ball non-sticky.

- Using a rolling pin (*belan*) roll out into an approx. 7" disc.
- Place the *paratha* on the pan and turn it over when bubbles start appearing (in about 1 minute).
- Spread ½ tsp ghee over the *paratha* and flip it over. Cook for 1 minute.
- Spread ½ tsp ghee over the *paratha* and flip it over. Cook for 1 minute. Now both sides should have been well oiled and cooked.
- Remove from pan and repeat the same process with remaining dough balls (you can start rolling out the second dough ball even as the first is still roasting. This, however, requires multi-tasking ability or else you will burn the *parathas*).

▸▸ Suggested Deployment

Parathas can be eaten with any vegetable, *dal* or curry dish.

ALOO PARATHA

Pan-fried Potato-stuffed Bread

Serves 2

High-Level Project Overview

Originated in North India, *aloo paratha* is a variant of plain *paratha*; it has a potato *masala* stuffing inside.

▸▸ Project Schedule

40 minutes in parallel execution mode

▸▸ Inventory & Procurement

4 cups / 600 gm Wholewheat (*atta*) flour
2 Potatoes, large
1 Onion, small
½ tsp / 2½ gm Red chilli powder
½ tsp / 2½ gm *Garam masala* powder
½ tsp / 2½ gm Turmeric (*haldi*) powder
½ cup / 30 gm Green coriander (*hara dhaniya*) leaves
1 tsp / 5 gm Salt
4 tbsp / 60 ml Vegetable oil / Ghee

▸▸ Quality Assurance

- If this is the first time you are making *aloo parathas*, the disc may not exactly turn out a circle. Don't worry about that, practice makes perfect.
- Wash potatoes and green coriander in running water.
- Wait for cooker to depressurize before opening.
- Store *aloo parathas* in a thermoware container lined with cloth or paper. The thermoware container keeps the *parathas* warm while the cloth or paper absorbs the steam preventing them from getting soggy.

▸▸ Execution

Subroutine 1 – Preparing aloo masala (15 minutes)

- Place potatoes with skin in a pressure cooker and pour enough water to cover.
- Cook the potatoes till 3 whistles and allow the pressure cooker to cool. Remove potatoes, peel and grate.
- Finely chop onion and mix with grated potatoes along with red chilli, *garam*

masala, and turmeric powders, green coriander, and salt. Set this *masala* aside.

Subroutine 2 – Preparing dough (5 minutes)

- Place the flour in a bowl and slowly add some water.
- Knead the mixture and keep adding little water, until a non-sticky dough forms.
- Transfer the dough into an airtight container and refrigerate for at least 15 minutes. As the dough is required to set, it is advised that you always make it 15 minutes before commencing cooking your meal.

Subroutine 2 – Preparing aloo paratha (25 minutes)

- Heat a griddle (*tawa*) on medium flame.
- Put some flour on a plate and set it near your work area. Call this Plate A.
- While the griddle is heating, make approx. 6-8 2" diameter balls of the dough.
- Take one ball and dust it with the flour on Plate A, rotate it so all sides are coated with dry flour. The purpose of this action is to make the dough ball non-sticky.
- Using a rolling pin (*belan*) roll out an approx.. 7" disc. Put an egg-sized amount of *aloo masala* in the middle, fold the dough over and roll out again to a 7-8" diameter disc.
- Place the *aloo paratha* on the griddle for 1 minute.
- Spread 1 tsp ghee over the *paratha* and flip it over. Apply ghee on the other side and repeat until the *paratha* is uniformly cooked on both sides.
- Remove from griddle and repeat the same process with remaining dough balls (you can start rolling out the second dough ball even as the first is still roasting. This, however, requires multi-tasking ability or else you will burn the *parathas*).

▸▸ Testing & Optimization

- You can experiment with the *aloo masala* by adding various spice powders such as cumin and coriander powders.

▸▸ Suggested Deployment

Aloo paratha can be eaten with pickle, *raita, matar rasedaar* (see p. 63) or *matar paneer* (see p. 61).

MOOLI PARATHA

Pan-fried Radish-stuffed bread | Serves 2

High-Level Project Overview

Originated in North India, *mooli paratha* is a variant of *aloo paratha*; with radish *masala* stuffing inside.

▸▸ Project Schedule

35 minutes in linear execution mode

▸▸ Inventory & Procurement

4 cups / 600 gm Wholewheat (*atta*) flour

4 White radish (*mooli*)

½ tsp / 2½ gm *Garam masala* powder

¼ cup / 15 gm Green coriander (*hara dhaniya*) leaves

1 tsp / 5 gm Salt

4 tbsp / 60 ml Vegetable oil / Ghee

½ tsp / 2½ gm Red chilli powder

▸▸ Quality Assurance

- When buying wheat flour, ensure you get a brand that does not bleach the flour.
- Wash peeled radish and green coriander in running water.
- Store *mooli paratha* in a thermoware container lined with cloth or paper. The thermoware container keeps the *parathas* warm while the cloth or paper absorbs the steam preventing them from getting soggy.

▸▸ Execution

Subroutine 1 – Preparing mooli *masala (10 minutes)*

- Grate the radish and squeeze out the water / juice. Keep this juice aside.
- Add salt to the radish and set aside for 10 minutes. Squeeze out the excess water/ juice (add this juice to the one already squeezed and saved above).
- Mix red chilli and *garam masala* powders, and green coriander to the radish; Set aside.

Subroutine 2 – Preparing dough (5 minutes)

- Place the flour in a bowl and slowly add some radish juice from Subroutine 1.
- Knead the mixture and continue to add radish juice (when you finish the radish juice start adding normal water) until a non-sticky dough forms.
- Transfer the dough into an airtight container and refrigerate for at least 15 minutes. As the dough is required to set, it is advised that you always make it 15 minutes before commencing cooking your meal.

Subroutine 3 – Preparing mooli paratha *(25 minutes)*

- Heat a griddle (*tawa*) on medium flame.
- Put some flour on a plate and set it near your work area. Call this Plate A.
- While the pan is heating, make approx. 6-8 2" diameter balls of the dough.
- Take one ball and dust it with the flour on Plate A, rotate it so all sides are coated with dry flour. The purpose of this action is to make the dough ball non-sticky.
- Using a rolling pin (*belan*) roll out an approx. 7" disc. Put a lemon-sized amount of radish *masala* in the middle, fold dough over and roll out again to a 7-8" diameter disc.
- Place the *mooli paratha* on the griddle for 1 minute.
- Spread 1 tsp ghee over the *paratha* and flip it over. Apply ghee on the other side and repeat until the *paratha* is uniformly cooked on both sides.
- Remove from the griddle and repeat the same process with remaining dough balls (you can start rolling out the second dough ball even as the first is still roasting. This, however, requires multi-tasking ability or else you will burn the *parathas*).

▸▸ Testing & Optimization

- You can experiment with the radish *masala* by adding various spice powders such as cumin and coriander powders. I have observed some women cook the radish *masala* in some oil before stuffing the *parathas* with it.

▸▸ Suggested Deployment

Mooli parathas can be eaten with pickle, *raita, dum aloo* (see p. 108), and vegetable kofta (see p. 43). As it has its own unique flavour, I recommend not serving it with strong flavoured dishes such as *sambar* or *vadia*-based dishes.

PURI

Wholewheat Puffed Bread

Serves 2

> **High-Level Project Overview**
>
> I guess a baker somewhere thought, 'Well, we have baked bread in ovens and we have roasted bread on pans, how else can bread be made?' This is classic 'fried' bread. Dough is kneaded into thin discs, deep-fried and eaten with curries. Favourite of the erstwhile Indian royalties who liked the breads deep-fried in ghee.

▸▸ Project Schedule

25 minutes in linear execution mode

▸▸ Inventory & Procurement

4 cups / 500 gm Refined flour (*maida*)

1 tsp / 5 gm Salt

4 cups / 800 ml Vegetable oil

▸▸ Quality Assurance

- Ensure flame is set to medium when frying, high flame will overheat the oil and burn the *puris* in a jiffy.
- Store the *puris* in a thermoware container to help them keep soft and warm

▸▸ Execution

Subroutine 1 – Preparing dough (5 minutes)

- Mix the flour, salt, and 2 tbsp oil in a bowl and then slowly add some water.
- Knead the mixture and continue to add a little water, at a time, until you get a non-sticky dough.
- Transfer the dough into an airtight container and refrigerate for at least 15 minutes. As the dough is required to set, it is advised that you always make it 15 minutes before commencing cooking your meal.

Subroutine 2 – Preparing puris *(20 minutes)*

- Heat the oil in a wok (*kadhai*) on medium flame.

- While the oil is heating, make approx. 8-10 1" diameter balls with the dough.
- Roll out each ball of dough with a rolling pin (*belan*) into an approx. 5" disc. Use a few drops of oil to stop it from sticking to the rolling pin.
- Carefully slip the *puri* into the oil and fry for about 30 seconds. It will rise to the top of the oil and turn brown when it is well cooked.
- Turn the *puri* over and, using the ladle, press it down into the oil so it puffs up.
- Remove the *puri* and place on a clean paper towel.
- Repeat the process with the remaining dough balls.

▸▸ Testing & Optimization

- You can replace the vegetable oil with ghee.
- In certain parts of India refined flour is replaced with wheat flour.

▸▸ Suggested Deployment

Puris can be eaten with *chana masala* (see p. 34) or *aloo matar rasedaar* (see p. 63).

MISSI ROTI

Fenugreek Flavoured Gram flour Bread

Serves 2

High-Level Project Overview

Originally invented by rural folks living in places where wheat does not grow, *missi roti* is either fully or partially made of gram flour (chickpea flour). In this recipe I have used 50-50 combination of wheat flour and gram flour. Due to the earthy nutty flavour of gram flour, this *roti* has a significantly different character than normal *roti* and should be served with curries that complement its flavour. When made fully with gram flour, *missi roti* does not have the same elastic body that wheat *roti* has due to less starch content in gram flour.

▶▶ Project Schedule

30 minutes in linear execution mode

▶▶ Inventory & Procurement

2 cups / 400 gm Wholewheat (*atta*) flour
2 cups / 300 gm Gram flour (*besan*)
1 bunch Fenugreek (*methi*) leaves
1 tsp / 5 gm Red chilli powder
¼ tsp Asafoetida (*hing*) powder
2 tbsp / 30 ml Vegetable oil
½ tsp / 2½ gm Salt
1½ tbsp / 25 gm Butter
2 cups / 500 ml Water, room temperature, or enough to make the dough

▶▶ Quality Assurance

- When buying wheat flour, ensure you get a good brand which does not bleach the flour.
- Sever any stems the fenugreek leaves have and wash in running water.
- Store the *missi roti* in a container which helps to keep it soft and warm.

▶▶ Execution

Subroutine 1 – Preparing dough (10 minutes)

- Finely chop the fenugreek leaves.
- Mix the wheat flour, gram flour, chopped fenugreek leaves, red chilli powder,

asafoetida, oil, and salt in a bowl. Slowly add some water. Knead the mixture and continue to add a little water, at a time, until you end up with a non-sticky dough.

- Transfer the dough into an airtight container and refrigerate for at least 30 minutes. As the dough is required to set it is advised that you always make it before commencing cooking your meal.

Subroutine 2 – Preparing missi roti (25 minutes)

- Heat a griddle (*tawa*) on medium flame.
- While the griddle is heating, make approx. 6-8 1" diameter balls from the dough.
- Take one ball, dust it with some dry wheat flour and roll out into an approx. 7" disc.
- Place the *missi roti* onto the griddle for 1 minute.
- Turn the *roti* when bubbles start appearing, using a pair of tongs to flip the *roti*.
- Now press the *roti* gently using a clean paper towel. The *roti* should puff up.
- Remove from griddle and repeat the same process with remaining dough balls (you can start rolling out the second dough ball even as the first is still roasting. This, however, requires multi-tasking ability or else you will burn the *rotis*).
- Remove the *roti* and dab a little butter on it to keep it soft.

▸▸ Testing & Optimization

You can experiment by replacing fresh fenugreek leaves with a variety of other spices such as dried fenugreek leaves (*kasoori methi*), dried coriander leaves or mint.

▸▸ Suggested Deployment

Missi rotis can be eaten with *dal makhni* (see p. 31), *lobiya masala* (see p. 40) or *Bharwan Shimla mirch* (see p. 119). As the *missi roti* has its own unique flavour, I do not recommend serving it with strong flavoured dishes such as *sambar*.

Raitas & Chutneys

KHIRA GAJAR RAITA

Cucumber and Carrot in Yoghurt

Serves 2

High-Level Project Overview

This yoghurt condiment originated from the need to maintain the Yin and Yang on the plate. Traditional Indian meals can be quite spicy and can cause the body to 'overheat'. The yoghurt base of this dish will balance off and neutralize the heating effect of the spices. In this recipe the yoghurt is flavoured with two very cooling vegetables – cucumber and carrot – with a hint of pepper.

▸▸ Project Schedule

15 minutes in linear execution mode

▸▸ Inventory & Procurement

2 cups / 450 gm Yoghurt (*dahi*)
1 Cucumber (*khira*)
1 Carrot (*gajar*)
1 tsp / 5 gm Salt
¼ tsp Black pepper (*kali mirch*)

▸▸ Quality Assurance

- When shopping for carrots and cucumbers, look for bright coloured ones, tight appearance and stiff bodies. Old carrots and cucumbers discolour, shrivel and lose their firmness (won't snap when bent).

▸▸ Execution

- Finely grate the cucumber and carrot. Set aside in a glass bowl.
- Using a whisk or spoon, thoroughly beat the yoghurt to a smooth consistency.
- Mix yoghurt, salt, and black pepper with grated cuccumber and carrot.
- Place in a serving dish and refrigerate until ready to serve.

⏩ Testing & Optimization

- You can add seasoning, if desired, of oil, red chilli powder, asafoetida, and curry leaves.

⏩ Suggested Deployment

This is an accompaniment to a meal and must be served in such capacity.

ALOO PYAZ RAITA

Potato and Onion Raita in Yoghurt

Serves 2

High-Level Project Overview

In South India, yoghurt is often flavoured with a variety of spice powders and served with meals. This recipe mixes these ingredients on a heavier base of potatoes and onions. The soft boiled potatoes and crisp onion pieces produce interesting textures making it a good accompaniment with rotis and curries. Add a couple of handfuls of boiled chickpeas to make this a self-sufficient tasty snack.

▶▶ Project Schedule

15 minutes in linear execution mode

▶▶ Inventory & Procurement

2 cups / 450 gm Yoghurt (*dahi*)

2 Potatoes, medium-sized

1 Onion, medium-sized

1 Green chilli

2 tsp / 10 gm Andhra peanut powder

▶▶ Quality Assurance

- Wash potatoes in running water before chopping.
- Wait for cooker to depressurize before opening.

▶▶ Execution

- Place potatoes with skin in pressure cooker with 1 tsp salt and pour enough water to cover. Pressure cook till 3 whistles. Remove potatoes, peel skin and chop into 1" cubes. Set aside. Finely chop the onion and green chilli.
- Using a whisk, thoroughly beat the yoghurt till it attains a smooth consistency.
- Mix the potatoes, onion, green chilli, and peanut powder in a bowl.
- Add the potato *masala* to yoghurt; mix thoroughly.
- Place in a serving dish and refrigerate until ready to serve.

▶▶ Suggested Deployment

This is an accompaniment to a meal and must be served in such capacity.

SHIMLA MIRCH RAITA

Sweet Capsicum in Yoghurt

Serves 2

High-Level Project Overview

This raita flavours yoghurt with a fantastic mix of bright multi-coloured capsicum and reverberating taste of ginger, all tied together with the aroma of roasted cumin. If you need a riot of vivid colours on your party table, then this dish is sure to please the eye and palate of your guests!

▸▸ Project Schedule

15 minutes in linear execution mode

▸▸ Inventory & Procurement

2 Capsicum, small, preferably yellow and red
2 cups / 450 gm Yoghurt (*dahi*)
1 tbsp / 15 ml Vegetable oil
2" piece Ginger (*adrak*)
¼ tsp Cumin (*jeera*) seeds
½ tsp / 2½ gm Salt

▸▸ Quality Assurance

- When buying capsicum, ensure that they are firm to touch and the skin is taut. Stems must be fresh and fleshy. Old capsicum will be shrivelled and de-hydrated.
- Scrape ginger with a knife to remove skin before chopping into pieces.

▸▸ Execution

- Slice the capsicum into thin strips, ensure to remove the seeds. Set aside.
- Finely chop the ginger. Set aside.
- Using a whisk or spoon, beat the yoghurt till it attains a smooth consistency.
- Dry roast cumin seeds in a pan on high flame for 2 minutes. Powder these in a mortar (if you do not have a mortar-pestle, place the roasted seeds on a tissue or paper, fold and press over with a rolling pin till the seeds are powdered).
- Heat the oil in a pan for 1 minute on high flame.

- Add capsicum slices, ginger, roasted cumin powder, and salt. Fry for 2 minutes and switch the flame off. Add capsicum *masala* to the yoghurt and mix well.
- Place in a serving dish and refrigerate until ready to serve.

►► Suggested Deployment

This is an accompaniment to a meal and must be served in such capacity.

PYAZ KI CHUTNEY

Onion Relish

Serves 4

High-Level Project Overview
Chutney is an Indian relish, often served on the side to enhance the taste of the main meal. In our first chutney recipe, we will explore a great way to make onions into a spicy tangy chutney that will go wonderfully well with hot rice and a dollop of ghee.

▸▸ Project Schedule

10 minutes in linear execution mode

▸▸ Inventory & Procurement

2 Onions, large

2 Green chillies

3" piece Ginger (*adrak*)

½ tsp / 2½ gm Salt

2 tsp / 10 ml White vinegar (*sirka*)

2 tbsp / 30 ml Vegetable oil

½ tsp Mustard seeds (*rai*)

2 tsp / 10 gm Tamarind (*imli*) paste

½ tsp / 2½ gm Turmeric (*haldi*) powder

1 tsp / 5 gm Red chilli powder

▸▸ Quality Assurance

- Scrape ginger with a knife to remove skin before chopping into pieces.
- Wash peeled onions, green chillies and ginger in running water.

▸▸ Execution

- Place onions, green chillies, and ginger in a blender and chop into fine pieces (do not make a paste).
- Sprinkle salt and vinegar and set aside.
- Heat the oil in a pan on high flame for 1 minute.
- Add mustard seeds and allow them to splutter.
- Add tamarind paste, turmeric and red chilli powders. Fry on medium flame for 1 minute, stirring constantly.
- Add the *masala* to the chopped onions with green chilli and ginger; mix well.

▸▸ Testing & Optimization

- I am adding vinegar in addition to tamarind as it lends the sharp edge of sourness, complementing the blunt earthy flavour of tartaric acid in tamarind.

▸▸ Suggested Deployment

This is an accompaniment to a meal and must be served in such capacity.

NARIYAL KI CHUTNEY

Coconut Chutney

Serves 4

High-Level Project Overview

This mild coconut based chutney is popularly served with dishes of higher pungency (like sambar) in South Indian breakfasts such as idli, upma and dosa. The coconut chutney is equally at ease in accompanying a hot mooli paratha with some pickle. In South India, this chutney is spiced up with either fried dry red chillies (my personal preference) or finely chopped raw green chillies.

▸▸ Project Schedule

10 minutes in linear execution mode

▸▸ Inventory & Procurement

1 Coconut (*nariyal*)
1 Green chilli
2 tbsp / 30 ml Vegetable oil
1 tsp / 3 gm Mustard seeds (*rai*)
2 Dry red chillies (*sookhi lal mirch*)
1 stalk Curry leaves (*kadhi patta*)
1 tsp / 5 gm Salt

▸▸ Quality Assurance

- Wash green chilli, curry leaves, and ginger in running water.

▸▸ Execution

- Break coconut and extract flesh. Using a small knife peel the outer hard brown layer attached to the white flesh.
- Place coconut and green chilli in a blender and blend to a paste. Add some water, if required, to bring to pasty consistency (or you can add the coconut water you must have saved in a cup when you broke the coconut open).
- Heat the oil in a pan on high flame for 1 minute.
- Add mustard seeds and allow them to splutter.
- Add dried red chillies and curry leaves. Fry for 30 seconds.
- Add seasoning to the coconut and green chilli paste; mix well.

⏩ Testing & Optimization

- Freshly grated coconut has a very mild flavour, if you experiment with the spices remember that the flavour of each experimental ingredient will come out strongly in the final result.

⏩ Suggested Deployment

This is an accompaniment to a meal and must be served in such capacity.

NIMBU KI CHUTNEY

Spicy Lemon Relish

Serves 4

High-Level Project Overview

This dangerously hot and sour chutney is on the border between chutney and a pickle. Guaranteed to bring vibrant life to any dull meal! I have put this chutney to many uses over the years as sandwich spread to *paratha* liner and rice mix. Whatever you eventually use it for, be prepared to sweat!

▶▶ Project Schedule

20 minutes in linear execution mode

▶▶ Inventory & Procurement

10 Lemons (*nimbu*)

1 tbsp / 15 ml Mustard (*sarson*) oil

1 tsp / 3 gm Mustard seeds (*rai*)

3" piece Ginger (*adrak*)

3 tsp / 15 gm Red chilli powder

½ tsp Asafoetida (*hing*) powder

2 tsp / 10 gm Salt

▶▶ Quality Assurance

- Wash and scrape ginger with a knife to remove skin before chopping into tiny pieces.
- Do not replace freshly squeezed lemon juice with supermarket ready made lemon juice. These generally have other additives that alter the taste.

▶▶ Execution

- Cut and extract juice from the lemons, filter to remove pulp and seeds. Set aside.
- Heat the oil in a saucepan on high flame for 1 minute.
- Add mustard seeds and allow them to splutter.
- Add ginger pieces and fry on medium flame for 1 minute.
- Add red chilli powder and asafoetida; fry further for 5 seconds.
- Add lemon juice and salt. Mix well and cook on low flame till the liquid is reduced to a thick paste.

▶▶ Testing & Optimization

- Adjust salt as desired.

▶▶ Suggested Deployment

This is an accompaniment to a meal and must be served in such capacity.

DHANIYA PUDINE KI CHUTNEY

Coriander Mint Chutney

Serves 4

High-Level Project Overview

Aromatic chutney made with coriander and mint leaves, this chutney is quite fragrant and is the primary chutney of choice for dipping in snacks such as samosa and pakoras. Traditionally spiced up with green chillies, it makes a perfect partner for an aloo paratha coated with ghee coming hot off the pan.

▶▶ Project Schedule

10 minutes in linear execution mode

▶▶ Inventory & Procurement

2 bunches Green coriander (*hara dhaniya*) leaves
1 bunch Mint (*pudina*) leaves
2 Green chillies, large
2 Lemons (*nimbu*)
1 tsp / 5 gm Salt

▶▶ Quality Assurance

- Remove coriander and mint leaves from stalks and wash in running water.

▶▶ Execution

- Cut and extract juice from the lemons, filter to remove pulp and seeds. Set aside.
- Place coriander, mint, and green chillies in a blender and blend to a smooth paste.
- Add salt and lemon juice.
- Chill in refrigerator before serving.

▶▶ Testing & Optimization

- In some variations, I have observed people adding standard tempering (*tadka*) to the coriander-mint paste.
- You can blanch the leaves in boiled water for 5 minutes before blending, to get greater consistency in the paste.

- This chutney is quite concentrated. If it's too spicy for your taste, dilute with more lemon juice before consuming.

Suggested Deployment

This is an accompaniment to a meal and must be served in such capacity.

About the author

KIRAN RAO has over a decade of international experience in various senior management positions working for blue chip companies in India, the United Kingdom and the United States. He holds an engineering degree in Electronics, is a certified Six Sigma Black Belt, PRINCE2 Practitioner, PMP and ITIL Green Badge.

He has been cooking Indian food since a young age and relishes traditional spicy food from Andhra Pradesh. Despite demanding work schedules, Kiran does not miss an opportunity to cook up a storm with flavours and spices.

Working in the IT industry, Kiran has come across many young engineers far away from home and struggling with life on their own. Unlike other vagaries of life, there is nothing quite like home-cooked food to make difficulties disappear. This book is an outcome of Kiran's decision to help young people cope with one of the most important experiences in life.